D1709293

SOCIAL STUDIES METHODS
in Elementary Education

Abalo Adewui

Central Michigan University

cognella™
academic publishing

Bassim Hamadeh, CEO and Publisher
Michael Simpson, Vice President of Acquisitions
Jamie Giganti, Managing Editor
Jess Busch, Senior Graphic Designer
John Remington, Acquisitions Editor
Brian Fahey, Licensing Associate
Kate McKellar, Interior Designer

First published in the United States of America in 2014 by Cognella, Inc.

Trademark Notice: Product or corporate names may be trademarks or registered trademarks, and are used only for identification and explanation without intent to infringe.

Printed in the United States of America

ISBN: 978-1-62131-385-4 (pbk) / 978-1-62131-386-1 (br)

www.cognella.com   800-200-3908

CONTENTS

Acknowledgments

I have taught Social Studies Methods for several years, during which I was able to see firsthand areas of learning that were lacking but at the same time were essential for education major students in my class. The areas of learning include knowledge about the nature and scope of social studies, developing instructional planning skills through unit planning, and developing democratic dispositions. It is important for pre-service teachers to be adequately prepared in those areas of learning to get them ready for their first teaching experience in K–8 schools. The content of this book is fairly straightforward. I have drawn on ideas and insights gained from previous works. I have referenced and acknowledged all whose ideas have been used as quotes or paraphrases; however, the bulk of the content in this book is based on and informed by my experience in teaching in general and specifically teaching elementary social studies for several semesters. If I have misquoted anyone, please let me know so I can make the appropriate correction in the next edition. I am thankful to my past and current students because they have been a great inspiration for me to write this book.

Many thanks to Cognella Academic Publishing who offered to publish my work.

Preface

Every semester, students come to my Elementary Social Studies Methods class with a vague knowledge of the nature and scope of social studies. I spend time to help students gain a better knowledge base in social studies by providing them definitions from multiple perspectives. I believe it is essential that every social studies method student is knowledgeable about what he or she is teaching. I also spend time working with students as they develop unit plans for instruction at given grade levels. I introduce them to action verbs and how to write learning objectives that aim at three domains of learning (cognitive, psychomotor, and affective). I have a resubmission policy whereby every student in my method class has the opportunity to redo and resubmit his or her unit plans to earn full credit. I believe the mastery of instructional planning skills should be reflected in well-written unit plans that students will use in real classrooms to maximize learning. I believe that it is essential for every social studies method student to understand the purpose of social studies and why it should be taught. Traditionally, the main purpose for teaching social studies is for testing, whereby each state prescribes what should be taught to prepare students for producing high test scores. It is essential for education students in my method class to teach social studies with more content than for testing purposes only. According to the National Council for Social Studies (NCSS–1992, 2003), the primary purpose of social studies is to help young people develop the ability to make informed and reasoned decisions for the public good as citizens of a culturally diverse, democratic society in an interdependent world. To achieve this purpose, social studies method instruction must provide learning opportunities that stimulate young children's cognitive, psychomotor, and affective domains. This book provides ideas, activities, and suggestions on how to achieve this broader purpose.

Introduction

Facts About Social Studies

Sometimes people have a vague idea about what social studies is. Some believe it is less rigorous academically. According to Michigan Law PA 596 of 2004, social studies is a part of the core academic curricula along with reading, writing, mathematics and science; it is defined as history, geography, economics, and American government. Michigan Law PA 596 mandates that social studies be taught to each child at each stage of his or her schooling. Many schools, however, are not following this law in their omission of including social studies instruction in kindergarten through second grade. Some Michigan districts are dictating social studies be taught only two times a week for 20 minutes so that reading and math can be taught for hours each day. Public Act 517 of 2008 restores social studies MME scores as qualifiers for Michigan Promise Scholarship Award and requires the full three credits of social studies, without the one-credit opt-out, to receive the award. The Partnership for 21st Century Skills, the nation's leading advocacy organization focused on infusing twenty-first century skills into education, identified civics, government, economics, history, and geography as core subjects, and also identified global awareness; financial, economic, business, and entrepreneurial literacy; and civic literacy as significant, emerging content critical to success in twenty-first century. Social studies is the catalyst for learning about government and the values of civic engagement; with help, children grow into the leaders of tomorrow. Social studies assists young people in developing the ability to make informed and reasoned decisions for the public good as citizens of culturally diverse, democratic society and as part of an interdependent and global economy. Social studies MEAP/MME testing is supported by four major content organizations in Michigan: The Michigan Center for Civic Education, The Michigan Council for Economic Education, The Michigan Geographic Alliance, and the Michigan Council for History Education. The Michigan Council for Social Studies also supports social studies MEAP/MME testing. Social studies MEAP is tested for sixth and ninth grade students in Michigan in October and the Michigan Merit Exam (MME) is tested for 11th grade students in March. Questions appearing on the MEAP or the MME are piloted in Michigan classrooms. Each question used is reviewed for ethnic, gender, geographic, and racial bias and the results from the pilot usage are

reviewed for validity and reliability. The social studies MEAP helps students gain a better understanding and use of our constitutional principles and the core democratic values.

Social studies education today faces several challenges:

- **Challenge #1.** If school systems move to the trimester schedule, they diminish the value and intent of the half-credit Economics and half-credit Civic requirements.
- **Challenge #2.** The reduction in professional development funds is restricting the professional training of Michigan K–12 teachers' significant need for Economics, Personal Finance, and Entrepreneurship education.
- **Challenge #3.** Inadequate economics requirements for undergraduate pre-service teachers are leaving them woefully deficient in their ability to adequately deliver quality economic education in the K–8 classrooms.
- **Challenge #4.** Many elementary and some middle school teachers lack depth of content knowledge to address the new history, geography, economics, and civics content expectations.
- **Challenge #5.** Social studies is a spiral curriculum with content expectations that were designed down from high school to middle school to elementary school. Skipping social studies instruction or reducing time dramatically in elementary school sets students and teachers in secondary schools up for a struggle if not failure.

Teaching is a process of facilitating learning; as such, it occurs in a variety of ways and in a variety of contexts. Any responsible social studies teacher's goal is to educate young people to make thoughtful decisions for the public good with the knowledge that civic competence is essential for the survival of our democratic way of life. While students are expected to be literate, to read and compute, they must also be democratically literate. We learn from research that students benefit from instruction if spatial thinking skills are given adequate consideration in the social studies curriculum, unit plans and lesson plans as early as in kindergarten and first-grade classrooms. In 21st century society, geography should be taught in the early grades using different methodologies.

In a social context that values standards and test scores over in-depth learning and creative endeavors, teaching is simply reduced to monitoring a fixed set of testable competencies whereby teachers tend to "teach to the test" with the hope that students will do well in the tests and help increase federal financial incentives to their schools. Likewise, when the main purpose of elementary school education is about mastering basic skills of reading, writing, and arithmetic (3Rs), it should be expected that in social studies classrooms, teachers will read stories from books that stressed citizenship virtues such as courage, honesty, fairness, and obedience in an effort to instill democratic virtues and patriotic pride in young citizens. This approach to teaching is characterized by a methodology of transmission of American cultural heritage and contributes to the maintenance of the status quo.

This methodology prevailed in the twentieth century but has been challenged thanks to new knowledge in psychology and science about teaching and learning. New expectations for learning outcomes for young Americans in the twenty-first century go beyond the basic skills and the methodology of transmission. The Partnership for the 21st Century Skills celebrates the methodology of transformation whereby learning outcomes are reflected in the young learner's ability to understand and explain human existence, and conduct research using different methodologies including: field investigations; living and working among people being researched; examining historical primary documents, artifacts, and records; creating and interpreting maps; administering tests and questionnaires; conducting interviews and surveys; and making decisions based on facts. Clearly this approach to teaching expands learning experiences for young children because, unlike the transmission approach, the transformation approach provides learning opportunities that stimulate the cognitive, psychomotor, and affective domains of learning in young children. The transformation methodology draws from Dewey's philosophy of education that maintains that the school is a context in which democracy as a social process could be learned. He contributed to a move away from describing curriculum in terms of subjects and blocks of time to planning and designing a curriculum that expanded the experiences of children. The National Society for the Study of Education (NSSE) adopted Dewey's ideas and further promoted the integration of history, geography, civics, and economics, which ultimately became known as social studies. Over the years many social studies textbooks have been written and adopted in social studies methods classes. These include titles such as "Social Studies for the Preschool-Primary Child" Seefeldt, Carol (1997); "Elementary Social Studies: A Practical Guide" Chapin, J.R. and Messick G.R. (1991); "Elementary and Middle School Social Studies: An Interdisciplinary Instructional Approach" Farris, J.P. (2001); "Social Studies for Children: A Guide to Basic Instruction" Michaelis, J.U. and Garcia, J. (1996); Welton, D.A. (2002). "Children and Their World: Strategies for Teaching Social Studies" McEachron, G.A. (2001). "Self in the World: Elementary and Middle School Social Studies." Boston: McGraw Hill. Maxim, G.W. (2003); Wolfinger, D.M. and Stockard, J.W. (1997). "Elementary Methods: An Integrated Curriculum." Longman. Johnson, A.P. (2010). "Making Connections in Elementary and Middle School Social Studies" Sage; Brophy, J. Alleman, J., and Halvorsen, A.L. (2013). "Powerful Social Studies for Elementary Students" Cengage. Zarillo, J. (2012).

My experience using readily available textbooks in my social studies methods classes is that there are so many chapters sometimes with redundant information. Consequently, there is the temptation to either cover all the chapters in the order they are presented in the book, spending less time on other chapters whereby students receive only a shallow information about the content of the chapter; or skipping some chapters altogether. Covering many chapters, spending less time on others or skipping chapters altogether is antithetical to meaningful and in-depth learning. One of the purposes of social studies education is to prepare and equip young individuals with knowledge of core democratic values, historical and current social issues impacting their daily lives, ability to distinguish between what is fact and opinion, what enhances the human condition and what does not, and decisions and judgment-making skills to lead qualitative lives within our global community. To effectively achieve the above-mentioned purposes, it is essential to streamline the content of social studies method books. Emphasis should be on the quality and less on the quantity; moreover the focus should be on the essential areas of learning. The essential areas of learning are learning outcomes expected for students in social studies methods class: they include gaining knowledge of social studies concepts and scope (cognitive), mastering instructional planning, research, inquiry and presentation skills, (psychomotor) and developing democratic dispositions within the framework of core democratic values. To effectively master these learning outcomes in a 16 week-long semester during which students take other courses concurrently such as language arts, reading, sciences, and technology where they are exposed to the same or similar teaching strategies. To escape or reduce redundancy, less is more.

Research also shows that when students are engaged in learning activities such as mock elections debates, classroom trials, and simulations, they are more likely to engage in the democratic process as adults. Historical perspective and context have always been an important facet of current decision-making. Teaching American and world history allows young people to gain a deeper understanding of the past through analysis and interpretation of historical events; they will then apply those skills to make informed decisions about the present. As a result of understanding history and the past, students will develop a better appreciation of our country and their individual roles and contributions as citizens for the common good. In the process of implementing insights from research, social studies teachers need to be aware of possible challenges that they may face. The challenges that most social studies teachers will face may be systemic and beyond their control. However, their commitment to educate young people to make thoughtful decisions for the public good with the knowledge that civic competence is essential for the survival of our democratic way of life should motivate them to face up to these challenges and guide their instructional decisions. Some of the challenges that social studies teachers will face include systemic practices that may be antithetical to best practices in social studies.

Images of learning in twenty-first century social studies method classes should reflect students engaged in learning activities including:

- Researching and documenting current events items from a newspaper.
- Undertaking historical inquiry projects using libraries and museums.
- Discussing and debating core democratic values.
- Engaging in civic actions and service-learning projects
- Writing reflections about accomplishment and growth and identifying areas of improvement.

The academic fields of sociology, anthropology, and psychology have not produced standards for the schools and therefore these three subject areas will not receive the same public attention as history, geography, civics, and economics in planning the curricula.

Organization of the Book

There are five parts to this book. The first is composed of five chapters, each focusing on one of the five areas of learning that are essential for students in social studies method courses.

- **Chapter 1** introduces students to the nature, scope, and definitions of social studies. It helps students in social studies methods class to develop an accurate knowledge base and understanding of social studies as a field, as a curriculum, as a theme, and as an interdisciplinary multidisciplinary subject.
- **Chapter 2** discusses the rationale and the purposes for teaching social studies in K–8 classrooms.

- **Chapter 3** describes how to develop instructional planning units and provides examples of unit plans for method students to be inspired and develop their own in order to master instructional planning skills.
- **Chapter 4** describes how to manage and monitor learning processes and provides ideas and suggestions on the management of learning in social studies classrooms to maximize instructional goals. Each suggestion and idea is supported and informed by insights gained from research and professional experience.
- **Chapter 5** describes how to design authentic and meaningful assessments and provides samples of assessment models that promote authentic learning and growth in the development of real life skills and dispositions expected of citizens in a democratic society.

Every semester, I have students in my Social Studies Methods class write individual reflections about what the class has meant to them as they move forward to become teachers. The most recurrent and thought-provoking comment from students revealed that they misconstrued social studies as a single subject, rather than a composite of subjects. This misconstruction is reflected in comments such as:

"I have always thought that social studies was the study of history and by learning about history we will hopefully not repeat history. I have now learned that is not the case and a social study is the study of "we and me", and discussing current events is social studies. I have also learned how to incorporate graphs and tables into socials studies mostly by taking polls/ surveys and displaying them in an interesting way."

"Learning in more details about what social studies actually is, including the definitions and concepts that contribute to social studies. I learned that social studies is not just history and what happened throughout the ages."

"I discovered through this class that there are far more aspects to social studies than just history and geography, and that student need to be exposed to all of them. So often those topics go untouched as teachers move about the traditional; curriculum of geography and history, through read aloud and not taking both of which are hardly effective methods of teaching a variety of learners anyway."

These comments informed me and justified my decisions to devote the first part of this book to the introduction of the nature and scope of social studies.

Historically, social studies has been an ongoing debate over its nature, scope and definition. Although many in the field seem to reduce social studies to one single or a list of subjects such as history, geography, economics and civics, others hold that social studies should be concerned about all things social. Consequently, social studies is a composite of all fields within the academic curriculum. In other words, social studies draws its content from different core academic contents. It is essential for students who have chosen the teaching profession to be exposed to different teaching methodologies—but more importantly, they need to gain a deeper understanding of the nature and scope of the topic they are going to teach.

The second part of the book discusses the purposes of teaching social studies. When asked, "What do you study?" any student can answer without hesitation if he or she is enrolled in classes with mathematics, science, English, French, or a business concentration. They do not need to provide additional explanation as to why they are studying those subjects. The underlying assumption is that they will graduate and become an English teacher or a science teacher or a nurse. Similarly, when asked, "What do you teach?" any instructor with mathematics, English, or health credentials will not need to provide further explanations about the nature of the subject matter. Traditionally it is implicitly understood that you can teach those subjects as they are part of the mainstream subjects held in high esteem as essential. It is also implicitly understood that the purpose for teaching those subjects is to prepare a workforce with expertise in those academic fields to assume professional roles in the government or private sectors. Norm referenced tests are used as means of measuring the abilities and selecting the best.

Social studies falls in the same category as above but with a difference. On the one hand, the subjects mentioned above are parts of the social studies education and therefore hold the similar purpose. On the other hand, social studies has a very clear and different purpose, and that is to prepare younger generations of Americans to be informed citizens who make reasoned decisions to make a difference in their own lives, their communities, and globally. Obviously a purpose couched like this needs to be fleshed out with details and examples in order to help people understand the underlying purpose of social studies as a subject that must be taught. Method students going in the teaching profession will be effective in the classroom only if they are able to define social studies and able to articulate why it is worth teaching. A student's ability to demonstrate his or her understanding of the nature of social studies and its purpose will help him or her to develop effective and meaningful instructional methodology to teach social studies.

The third part of the book describes how to teach social studies. Knowing the definition of social studies and understanding its purposes and importance are essential pre-requisites for students to know prior to tackling how to teach social studies. There is no one method, lesson format, and unit plan for everyone to follow. As a matter of fact with a subject so vast in scope and so complex, it would be shortsighted and unrealistic to expect or mandate one single instructional planning format for everybody to follow. However, having made the case for diversity in methodology and instructional planning formats, one needs to be reminded that while you can use a lesson format or unit plan that is different from a suggested format, your format must contain the same number of steps to follow to complete a lesson plan. Obviously, students should be encouraged to develop a lesson plan that fits their teaching style.

The essential components or steps in a standard lesson plan include:

- The demographic information: title of the lesson, grade level, date, name of the school, curriculum focus
- The grade level content expectations
- The knowledge/ learning objectives
- Teaching materials
- Modeling
- Lesson delivery
- Closure

One of the assumptions throughout this book and in social studies in general is that in-depth learning is valued. Similarly, with respect to the interdisciplinary nature of social studies, more attention should be given to developing unit plans instead of single stand-alone lesson plans where learning is shallow. Obviously, a unit plan is made of single but connected lesson plans. Each social studies lesson is about a theme, a concept that is not fully understood within a thematic unit plan. An effective social studies lesson plan must contain the following:

- Demographic information
- Grade level content expectations
- Knowledge outcomes
- Skill outcomes
- Dispositions
- Learning Activities
- Closure

As students in the Social Studies Method course become familiar with the nature and scope of the field, as they develop a good understanding of the purpose, and as they demonstrate a satisfactory mastery of instructional planning skills, they are now ready to implement their plan in the classroom.

The fourth part of the book provides useful suggestions for classroom teaching and provides insights, ideas, and suggestions on how to effectively manage the classroom to maximize learning. The key to successful teaching is the ability to manage learning in the classroom.

In theory, after following the steps discussed in the first three parts of the book, teaching should sail smoothly. This is rarely the case in practice because of the unpredictable nature of the classroom. You must always expect the unexpected. In a social studies classroom, there are four teaching strategies that need to be emphasized throughout the instruction:

- The learning activities must be meaningful to students. Students should be able to relate to the issue(s) being discussed in the lesson. They should be able to make connections with what they already know about the issue in another context. You must also teach to the objectives you stated in your lesson.
- The learning activities must be challenging. It is important to sequence your questioning techniques in line with Bloom's taxonomy. For example, your questions should not focus only on the cognitive domain of learning, knowledge. You should vary and range your questions from simple to complex. Or to use Bloom's hierarchy, you may ask knowledge questions as well as comprehension, application analysis, synthesis and evaluation questions—questions that stimulate students' interest in the lesson not because they are easy to answer but because they are challenging students to use their thought process to come up with an answer. The answer may not be right, though it most certainly may not be wrong either because in social studies, there are no right or wrong answers. There are thoughtful and thought-provoking and factual-based arguments. In social studies instruction, students are prepared to be good debaters about issues, concepts and theories. For example, the discussion about the core democratic values help students understand how people debate issues and come up with decisions. The goal here is to challenge students' beliefs and biases whereby they can develop tolerance and openmindedness.
- The learning activities should be value based. The question is, do we or should we teach values? Whose values would they be? Fortunately, the core democratic values play an essential role in the social studies classroom. The more you use them to stimulate discussions, the more interested students can be.

- Finally, students should be actively involved in the lesson at hand through the completion of activities in pairs or teams of three. When students are fully engaged in learning, there are less classroom management issues to deal with.

The fifth part of the book discusses different forms of assessments and their purposes and offers suggestions on how to develop your own assessment. Traditionally, there are two types of assessments: one is known as formative assessment because it is supportive and the goal is to help the students reach the learning outcome(s) expected. Teachers give formative assessments every day; in teaching, context assessment is embedded in the lesson because it looks at the progress students are making in the process of achieving the expected learning outcomes. The lesson sails smoothly when the progress is being made across the board. Lack of progress means the teacher needs to slow down the pace of the lesson and re-teach or explain what is not understood. It is called the embedded assessment. The other form of assessment is called the summative assessment or evaluation.

Unlike the formative, the summative assessment or evaluation is a value judgment on the work of students after a period of time or at the conclusion of a topic. Students get grades in points or percentages or as a letter grade. Ideally, every student in a given class should earn a full credit after the evaluation of their work because it assumed that they were able to master expected learning outcomes through formative or embedded assessment.

While both assessments are familiar in social studies, there is another form of assessment that is emphasized in social studies: the authentic assessment. Any assessment that is based on practices and skills needed in real life outside the classroom is an authentic assessment.

Whatever form of assessment is used, it is critical that it is consistent with the learning outcomes that are stated in the lesson. An effective assessment must reflect the learning outcomes and the activities. If the learning outcome is to show a mastery of one particular skill at the end of the class, then the activities during which the students practice the skills should be reflected in the assessment plan. Assessment is necessary to know what students are learning, if they are learning and how much they are learning. It is also necessary because it helps to see if all students are learning and, if they are not, what is causing them not to learn.

It is my hope that insights gained from reading each of the five parts of the book will pave the way to a successful, exciting social studies teaching experience.

CHAPTERS

Nature and Scope of Social Studies

Introduction

Students in my Social Studies Method class are prospective K–12 teachers. Therefore it is important for them not only to understand the nature and scope of the subject matter they are going to teach, but they must be able to articulate and define what social studies entails. They should also be able to highlight the common purpose among the multiple definitions of social studies and the implications for teaching.

Defining Social Studies

Social studies has been part of elementary curriculum for decades, yet it is not an easy subject to define. To begin with, it is essential to consider the difference between the terms "social science" and "social studies." The word "science" is derived from the Latin word *scientia*, which means knowledge. Therefore social science may be defined as any of the fields that seek to understand and explain the social realm of human existence. These include geography, history, political science, sociology, anthropology, and economics. To understand and explain human existence, social scientists conduct research using different methodologies including field investigations; living and working among people being researched; examining historical documents, artifacts, and records; creating and interpreting maps; administering tests and questionnaires; and conducting interviews and surveys (Maxim, 2003).

Definition 1

According to Maxim (2003), the main purpose of elementary school education was focused on basic skills of reading, writing, and arithmetic (3Rs). In social studies classrooms, teachers read stories from books that stressed citizenship virtues such as courage, honesty, fairness, and obedience to instill democratic virtues and patriotic pride.

Definition 2

According to Michaelis, J.U. and Garcia, J. (1996), social studies is the area of the curriculum that transmits basic aspects of our cultural heritage (subject-matter centered). It provides instruction on thinking and decision-making skills applied to social problems (society centered). It provides instruction to develop the competencies needed for social criticism and action (society centered). It develops students' potential for self-directed participation in group activities (student centered).

Definition 3

Wilma Robles de Melendez, Vesna Beck, Melba Fletcher (2000) defined social studies as an area of study with boundless educational possibilities. As an academic field, social studies includes many different areas of study, ranging from geography and environmental science to art and current events among others. It is necessary to include them in the early childhood curriculum. A good background in social studies in the early years can provide a social foundation on which later education in history, civic responsibility, and character development can be built.

Definition 4

According to the National Council for Social Studies (NCSS 1992, 2003), social studies is the integrated study of the social sciences and humanities to promote civic competence. It provides coordinated, systematic study drawing upon such disciplines as anthropology, archeology, economics, geography, history, philosophy, political sciences, psychology, religion, and sociology as well as appropriate content from humanities, mathematics, and natural sciences. The primary purpose of social studies is to help young people develop the ability to make informed and reasoned decisions for the public good as citizens of a culturally diverse, democratic society in an interdependent world.

Definition 5

Social studies is more than a collection of facts for children to memorize. It is an understanding of how people, places, and events came about and how people can relate and respond to each other's needs and desires, as well as how to develop respect for different viewpoints and cultural beliefs. It is the study of cultural, economic, geographic, and political aspects of past, current, and future societies (Farris, J.P. 2001).

Definition 6

Social studies is the study of things social (John Dewey, 1938).

Definition 7   Social studies is an area of the curriculum deriving its goals from the nature of citizenship in a democratic society with links to other societies. Drawing its content from social science and other disciplines, it also incorporates the personal and social experiences of students and their cultural heritage. It links factors outside the individual, such as cultural heritage, with factors inside the individual, particularly the development and use of reflective thinking, problem solving, and rational decision-making skills for the purpose of creating involvement in social action (Sunal, C.S.; Haas, M.E., 1993).

The working definition of social studies adopted in this book is a combination of all seven definitions that gives a holistic view of the purposes of social studies. Approaching social studies instruction from a holistic perspective allows for a comprehensive selection and implementation of social issues, topics, and themes including core democratic values, the NCSS themes, current events, education, health, economics, history, geography, environment, hunger, poverty, bullying, religion, relationships, and politics. This is captured in John Dewey's (1938) definition: "Social studies is the study of things social." Clearly, social studies encompasses everything social.

Perspectives on Social Studies

On the one hand there was the old philosophy that advocated transmission of knowledge and social expectations in order to assimilate the new immigrants into the American society. On the other hand the NEA advocated teaching for social transformation whereby new immigrants are prepared to face the challenges and expectations of the new society. They need to be able to transform and create new knowledge for themselves in the new society. The role of the school was not simply to prepare people to recall facts or checklists of procedures in response to specific stimuli. Instead the school was to guarantee social efficiency by educating young people to understand and resolve social problems. This philosophy was advocated by leading educators such as Francis Parker and John Dewey, and its main goal for school was to make school subjects practical so they are conducive to meaningful learning. One of these new school subjects became known as social studies. The subject matter or content for this newly introduced school subject was to be drawn from the most popular social sciences of the time: history, geography, and political science, often referred to as civics. Blended together as one school subject, it filled the need to help young people understand our American heritage and acquire the skills basic to positive participation in the nation's democratic process.

Obviously, as might be expected with every sensitive educational issue, not everyone shared this view of the role of the school, or for that matter, welcomed the new subject called social studies. People always have strong opinions about what knowledge or whose knowledge is the best and worthwhile. However, after years of controversy, that might still be lingering. The underlying purpose of social studies stemming from the NCSS definition is the education for citizenship within the framework of an integrated curriculum that encompasses content from social sciences such as history, geography, and civics. It also recommends a methodology that promotes higher-order thinking skills over rote memorization of facts. Also of high importance is decision making and personal responsibility as attributes for good citizenry; the survival of democratic ideals depends on a citizenry that cares for its country and for humanity as a whole.

Operationally, social studies instruction should prepare young people to become good citizens: individuals possessing the knowledge, skills, and attitudes required to participate in and preserve our democratic society. Good citizens respect the American past as a democratic society and ac-knowledge the contributions of all ethnic groups who have made America a powerful country. Good citizens take active roles as champions of freedom and hold people accountable for the responsibilities of citizenship. Good citizens speak up, take action, and vote for the improvement of the quality of life in their families, neighborhood, community, nation, and the world. Good citizens volunteer in civic or public realms. Good citizens take part in real problem solving. It is critical for social studies educators to teach these ideals to young people in order to secure and preserve democracy.

This premise, of course, breaks from the traditional teaching of social studies that views teaching as a transmission of a body of knowledge from a book or a teacher, and learning as the passive absorption of this knowledge. Operating within the framework this premise requires a shakeup of the traditional mindset about teaching and learning.

Engage Students in Meaningful Tasks

Children are naturally curious. They want to know the why of things; they want to touch, smell, and do things. Children should be given the opportunity to explore and develop their own understand-ing of the world around them just like the professional scientists, historians, geographers, and political scientists.

It is the responsibility of future teachers to embrace the new methodology for teaching social studies that is deemed necessary for readying young people for the twenty-first century. They must create classroom environments that promote process of data gathering, discussions, decision mak-ing, cooperation, curriculum integration, and diverse perspectives.

Philosophies of education are important because they provide direction for what teachers do and help explain why learners do what they do. Philosophies grow out of the ideas we gain through experience and theories established by scholars in given field. Take a moment to check on your goals for your students. List at least four. Are your goals similar or different from your state, district, and school? Make the work of your students visible. Display their work and promote public recogni-tion and appreciation for excellence.

Over the years the content of the elementary curriculum has expanded to meet and keep pace with the social ethos, demographic shifts, and new research findings about teaching and learning.

Consequently a greater sociocultural understanding, an attitude of care and concern, a willingness to participate in social criticism and critical self-reflection, and a commitment to engage in personal actions that serve an increasing number of others (Houser, 1999).

Social studies today seems to be tied to social disciplines. In other words, the core subjects of history, geography, and civics have expanded to include all the social sciences disciplines that were singled out and taught in isolation. Likewise teachers are expected to teach content areas in depth and in scope by integrating other content areas.

When goals are couched as such with expectations to teach for in-depth understanding and breadth, it becomes legitimate for social studies teachers to wonder how these goals can realistically be met in one subject area when operationally social studies is only one aspect of the entire school day. As one teacher put it, "we have curricular obesity and everyone wants to add more" (McEachron, 2001, p. 9).

In 1966, the Social Sciences Education Consortium developed and joined the fundamental ideas or structures of economics, political sciences, sociology, anthropology, and geography. The structures were expected to be part of the teacher education programs as they have become the core content in social studies for several decades. The concepts seem to overlap from one subject to another.

Hence, combining the same concepts that many subject matters address would lead to a multidisciplinary approach. For example, a thematic unit plan on families would incorporate concepts from history, economics, political sciences, sociology, anthropology, geography, and psychology.

Social studies is the integrated study of the social sciences and humanities to promote civic competence. It provides coordinated, systematic study, drawing upon such disciplines as anthropology, archeology, economics, geography, history, philosophy, political sciences, psychology, religion, and sociology, as well as appropriate content from humanities, mathematics, and natural sciences.

Citizenship Transmission (Socialization)

Commitment to democratic values—"The American Creed," national unity (James Shaver)—Recitation of the pledge of allegiance; singing patriotic songs; retelling stories and legends about historic figures; celebrating birthdays of presidents; etc. Films and literature help to invoke in students positive feelings about their heritage. The danger is this can lead to indoctrination: the shaping of students' minds by providing information without allowing questions or a critical view.

Cooperative Learning (Farris Cooper)

- Noncompetitive

- Stimulates student interactions
- Contribution highly expected from individual members
- Critical social skill
- Hours of interactive learning
- Empowers students
- Places responsibility for learning on students

Cooperative or Collaborative Learning (Chapin, J.R. and Messick, G.R.)

- Students work together in small groups on a common topic or problem
- Exchange and evaluate data, ideas
- Learn or review new material
- Learn from their peers, improve intergroup relations.
- Viable instructional method to use to deliver content and teach skills
- Individual accountability
- Allows no free ride

Inquiry process/problem solving student-centered instruction vs. teacher-centered instruction (lecture to present information; recitation to test orally retained information).

Interdisciplinary/integrative approach to social studies as an interdisciplinary unit/lesson plan makes room for integrating content area. Large blocks of time for completing tasks in social studies requirements vary from state to state.

Collaborative Lesson/Unit Planning

Social studies should prepare students for problem solving. They should be engaged in tasks involving deep thought and action to find solutions to the problem. Problems require that existing knowledge be used to resolve new emerging problems (Turner, 2004). Intrinsic to problem solving is the ability to deal in constructive ways with failure and inability to identify easy or quick solutions. Problem-solving skills are perhaps the most pervasive of skills needed in life. In order to meet the future, students must develop the requisite mindset and attitudes needed in problem solving. In other words teachers should strive to prepare students to become problem solvers. A person with a problem-solving mindset will be successful in life; because to live is to solve problems. It is important for teachers to emphasize this concept in their classroom if they expect children to become independent, decision-making citizens.

Social studies has most often been regarded as an area that should be taught only if there is time. Priority time in the school day has been given to the essentials subjects such as reading, math, and language. The society, administrators, and teachers see reading, math, and language as basics, fundamental, or essentials that need priority attention.

Historically, the subject of history has taken precedence over geography. People had to be around before there could be history. History was the stories of the past about people. Geography came into being later and was about things like locating good hunting and fishing areas and avoiding places where water sources dried up in hot weather.

Gaining knowledge in geography was essential for survival. Both history and geography were very basic but essential. History helped people identify who they were, individually and collectively, and where they had come from. This is still true today because it is essential for young students to know and understand how things came to be and predict the future. Citizenship education on the other hand aims to provide children with the knowledge, skills, and dispositions that permit them to participate actively in a democratic society.

The focus on only academic subjects in teaching is a form of academic arrogance because all disciplines focus on the same thing (Welton, 2002). The notion of multidisciplinary, interdisciplinary, integrated social studies is limited to three nations: USA, Canada, and Australia. Everywhere else history and geography are taught separately.

Social studies is more than a collection of facts for children to memorize. It is an understanding of how people, places, and events came about and how people can relate and respond to each other's needs and desires, as well as how to develop respect for different viewpoints and cultural beliefs. It is the study of cultural, economic, geographic, and political aspects of past, current, and future societies. One of its purposes is to prepare children to become citizens of a democratic society. The field of social studies is uniquely suited to prepare children with the knowledge, skills, and attitudes they need to participate in and contribute to the small democracies of their homes, their schools, immediate neighborhoods today, as well as to become functioning citizens of society in general in the future. Seefeldt, Carol (1997).

Scope of Social Studies

What is social studies? According to Welton (2002) this question helps instructors define the scope of and sequence in social studies. A social studies instructor may, for example, begin with the fundamental question of what to teach. It would be naive to focus on one particular domain over the others. For example, an instructor may choose to focus on history, economics, or civics. As a matter of fact it is tempting to focus on one domain of knowledge that the instructor feels passionate about and comfortable to discuss with his or her students. In practice it is essential to teach each subject in connection with one another because they are interrelated. For example, teaching history, you can talk about people, places, geography, economics, and culture. Social studies as a field derives its content primarily from history, the social sciences, the humanities, and science. It is taught in ways that reflect an awareness of the personal, social, and cultural experiences and developmental levels of learners (National Council for the Social Studies Task Force on Scope and Sequence, Social Education, 1984).

The What, Why, and How are basic questions that must inform and guide social studies instructional decisions at any grade level. According to Welton (2002) these questions help instructors define their scope and sequence in social studies. Progressive social studies instructors may, for example, begin with the fundamental question of what to teach. Social studies, especially, encompasses several domains of knowledge from social science and humanities. It would be naive to focus on one particular domain over the others.

Over the years much has been written about social studies such as "Social Studies for the Preschool-Primary Child" Seefeldt, Carol (1997); "Elementary Social Studies: A Practical Guide" Chapin, J.R. and Messick G.R. (1991); "Elementary and Middle School Social Studies: An Interdisciplinary Instructional Approach" Farris, J.P. (2001); "Social Studies for Children: A Guide to Basic Instruction" Michaelis, J.U. and Garcia, J. (1996); Welton, D.A. (2002); "Children and Their World: Strategies for Teaching Social Studies" McEachron, G.A. (2001); "Self in the World: Elementary and Middle School Social Studies" Maxim, G.W. (2003); and "Dynamic Social Studies for Elementary Classrooms" Maxim, G.W. (2003).

From Jarolimek, J. (1990) "Social Studies in Elementary Education": "One does not inherit the culture through genetic transmission; the culture has to be transmitted through teaching and learning from one generation to the next or it is lost" (p. 5). It is important that all human species provide opportunities for their youth to learn the social and cultural imperatives that characterize their particular way of life to perpetuate and maintain continuity. Schools must assume the responsibility for the transmission of culture, knowledge skills, attitudes, and values that are deemed important or essential.

Social studies is a basic subject of the K–12 curriculum that draws its content primarily from history, the social sciences, and in some respects, from the humanities and sciences, and is taught in ways that reflect an awareness of the personal, social, and cultural experiences and developmental levels of learners (National Council for the Social Studies Task Force on Scope and Sequence, Social Education, 1984). The major mission of social studies education is to help children learn about the social world in which they live and develop skills, attitudes, and knowledge to act on solving problems to improve their social world. Social studies focus on citizenship education, which means learning to participate in group life (Jarolimek, 1990). Social studies aim at attaining two sometimes contradictory ends. On the one hand, socialization, through which citizens internalize values and attitudes that cause them to behave willingly in accordance with prevailing expectations and norms. This is a basic requirement for orderly social life. On the other hand, citizens in a free society also have the obligation to be critical of the system itself in order that basic rights and freedoms can be sustained and extended to all citizens through social criticism. The exercise of social criticism is crucial in a free society in order to prevent the erosion of rights and civil liberties guaranteed to all citizens by the Constitution. Teaching socialization and social criticism can pose a challenge. On the one hand, we want citizens to obey the law, but we do not want them to be intimidated by the law or those who enforce the law. We want citizens to support elected officials but we do not want them to blindly follow the leadership of demagogues. Teachers must find a balance between the two expectations when teaching civics at elementary and middle levels.

Social Studies as a Multidisciplinary and Interdisciplinary School Subject

As a multidisciplinary and interdisciplinary school subject, social studies is based primarily on history and social sciences disciplines. Historically, the subject of history has taken precedence over geography. People had to be around before there could be history. Geography came into being later and was about things like locating good hunting and fishing areas and avoiding places where water sources dried up in hot weather. Knowing geography was essential for survival. Both history and geography were very basic and essential. History helped them identify who they were, individually and collectively, and where they had come from.

Social Studies as Themes

Social studies as a field encompasses a variety of subjects but for teaching purposes, these subjects are broadly organized in ten thematic strands known as themes of social studies.

The Themes of Social Studies

1. Culture:	The study of culture and diversity equips students with a deeper understanding of how human beings create, learn, share, and adapt to their culture. Students learn to appreciate the role of their culture in shaping their lives and the lives of others. Culture as a theme is typically addressed in courses including geography, history, sociology, anthropology, and multicultural education.
2. Time, Continuity, and Change:	The study of the past and its legacy prepares students to be able to examine the institutions, values, and beliefs of people in the past. Using historical inquiry and interpretation, they develop a deeper understanding of how important historical events have shaped the modern world. This theme is addressed in history.

3. People, Places, and Environments:

The study of people, places, and environments helps students to develop their spatial views and perspectives of the world; to understand where people, places and resources are located and why. Students may explore the relationship between human beings and the environment. The study of people, places, and environments appears in geography.

4. Individual Development and Identity:

The family, peers, culture, and institutional influences are factors that shape personal identity. This theme is addressed in courses including psychology, anthropology, and sociology.

5. Individuals, Groups, and Institutions:

Institutions such as families and civic, educational, governmental, and religious organizations help shape people's lives. The study of this theme helps students gain a deeper understanding of how institutions are formed, maintained, and changed through the examination of their influences. This theme is usually addressed in courses including government, history, civics, law, and politics.

6. Power, Authority, and Governance:

The study of this theme provides insights and deeper understanding of the historical development and contemporary forms of power, authority, and governance. Students become knowledgeable about the purposes and functions of government, the scope and limits of authority, and the differences between democratic and non-democratic political systems. This theme usually appears in courses on government, history, civics, law, and politics.

7. Production, Distribution, and Consumption:

This theme is about the study of how people organize the production, distribution, and consumption of goods and services. It prepares students for the study of domestic and global economic issues. This theme is addressed in courses on economic concepts and issues.

8. Science, Technology and Society:

When students explore the relationships among science, technology, and society, they develop a deeper understanding of the past and present progress in science and technology and their impact on human life. This theme is typically addressed in courses including history, geography, economics, civics, and government.

9. Global Connections and Interdependence:

The study of this theme helps to prepare students to study and understand issues stemming from global phenomena. It is typically addressed in courses including geography, culture, economics, political science, government, and technology.

10. Civic Ideals and Practices: The main purpose of social studies is the promotion of civic competence; i.e., the knowledge, intellectual processes, and democratic dispositions required of students to be active and engaged in public life. This theme enables students to learn about the rights and responsibilities of citizens of a democracy and appreciate the importance of active citizenship. This theme is typically addressed in courses including civics, history, political science, cultural anthropology, global studies, and humanities.

All the themes are interrelated and therefore can be addressed in one or more of the subjects encompassing socials studies. The National Council for Social Studies (NCSS) developed standard themes for comprehensive learning expectations. For example, you can use the theme Time, Continuity, and Change when teaching history or geography; theme People, Places, and Environments to teach geography or natural science. For practical purposes, standards are developed at the state level around specific subjects that make up the learning expectations at each grade level, K–12. For example, in the state of Michigan, there are standards for grade-level content expectations (GLCEs) in K–8 social studies; the content includes history, geography, economics, civics, and government. Obviously each state may have its own standards and learning expectations.

Purposes of Social Studies

Introduction

The major mission of social studies education is to help children learn about the social world in which they live and develop skills, attitudes, and knowledge to act on solving problems to improve their social world. Social studies focus on citizenship education, which means learning to participate in group life (Jarolimek, 1990). Social studies aim at attaining two sometimes contradictory ends. On the one hand, the socialization through which citizens internalize values and attitudes that cause them to behave willingly in accordance with prevailing expectations and norms. This is a basic requirement for orderly social life. On the other hand, citizens also have the obligation to be critical of the system itself in order that basic rights and freedoms can be sustained and extended to all citizens through social criticism.

Social Purpose

Teaching socialization and social criticism can be a challenge. On the one hand we want citizens to obey the law, but we do not want them to be intimidated by the law or those who enforce the law. Citizens in a democratic society are expected to support individuals whom they have elected into office. At the same time citizens have a responsibility to hold accountable their elected officials and not follow them blindly when their leadership turns into demagoguery. Teachers must find a balance between the two expectations when teaching citizenship at the elementary and middle levels. If our goals are to prepare young people to acquire skills and operate like social scientists such as anthropologists, historians, and what have you, we must first acquire skills and knowledge about the roles of historians and geographers in order to make adequate methodological and instructional decisions in teaching social studies.

For example, anthropologists study people to find out about their physical, social, and cultural development; geographers study people and places, the natural environment, and the relationship with people living in these places. Their task is to locate, describe, and explain the physical characteristics (climate, vegetation, soil, and landforms) and their implications for human activity and existence.

The knowledge in geography helps us to manage the world's resources; historians research, analyze, and interpret the past. They use many sources of information including interviews, government records, newspapers, artifacts, photographs, diaries, letters, historic buildings, and sites. Traditionally, history has been a principal discipline contributing to social studies but it is not itself considered by many to be a true social science because the processes of empirical research are not rigorous in historical study. They reconstruct events of the past from available evidence that leads to interpretations that are not always accurate.

For example, in the 1920s, historians believed that the first large constructions in the world were the Egyptian pyramids. This contention was disproved in the 1960s with the introduction of the technique of carbon-14 dating, which indicated that northern European monuments such as Stonehenge were constructed earlier than most of the pyramids. Political scientists study the origin, development, and operation of political systems and public policy.

Civic inquiry, for example, is the study of the structure and functions of government; that is, how people get elected and what their duties are toward citizens. Political scientists conduct research on the relationship between the United States and other countries, the political life of nations, the politics of small towns, and decisions of the Supreme Court. They analyze the political institutions or policies and how they operate on a daily basis. The methodology includes poll taking, public opinion surveys, analyses of election results, interviewing of public officials, examining speeches of politicians, and studying the actions of judges.

Sociologists study society and social behavior by examining the groups and social institutions people form such as the family, government, religion, business, or school. Sociologists investigate the values and norms of groups to understand why group members behave the way they do. They interview group members; they observe the group or live with the group for a short time. The results of sociological research inform educators, lawmakers, and administrators in their efforts to solve social problems and formulate public policy.

Economists study the production, distribution, and consumption of goods and services. They try to understand how to satisfy unlimited wants with limited resources. Historically, social studies has come into being as a subject as a result of social changes that were noted in 1916 with new waves of immigrants who were looking for employment in the country's industry. To meet the needs of the new industrial economy of the nation, the National Education Association (NEA) proposed new approaches to teaching.

Global Purpose

NCSS (1979): The purpose of social studies is to prepare young people to be humane, rational, participating citizens in a world that is becoming increasingly interdependent. This statement is the dominant view of social studies. It defines the overall goal of social studies as citizenship education. Citizenship means active participation in community and national decision making (Goodman, Alder, 1985; Barr, Barth Shermis, 1977).

While there seems to be an agreement on the overall goal of social studies as citizenship education, some may place emphasis on a particular content.

While it is essential to write about the multiple purposes of social studies, it is more essential for practical and teaching purposes to clearly articulate the main purpose for teaching social studies. Why is it at all important?

According to the National Council for Social Studies (NCSS): "The primary purpose of social studies is to help young people make informed and reasoned decisions for the public good as citizens of a culturally diverse, democratic society in an interdependent world." Operationally defined, the objective of social studies is the promotion of civic competence, which is knowledge and making sense of new information and skills (actively processing the information and developing democratic dispositions). The learning expectations for students is that they are active and engaged participants in public life in their communities.

Clearly civic competence is the ultimate and essential goal for teaching social studies.

American Core Democratic Values

The American core democratic values are the fundamental beliefs and constitutional principles of American society, which unite all Americans. These values are expressed in the Declaration of Independence, the United States Constitution, and other significant documents, speeches, and writings.

To effectively implement the civic mission of social studies in K–12 classrooms—in other words to engage students in democratic citizenry—the instructional process should focus on stimulating students' interest in civic discourse through debate and discussions, problem-solving activities, inquiry, research, and social action through service learning. The discussions, debates, and social actions that students will be engaged in should be informed by the core democratic values because they provide the essential frame of reference for all discussions and debates that occur in a social studies classroom.

Unlike the traditional subjects that focus on knowledge that is measured by test scores, social studies goes beyond content knowledge. Social studies instruction should help students make sense of new information (knowledge), actively process the information (skills), and develop dispositions (values). Engaging students in discussions that draw from core democratic values helps them to develop democratic dispositions that are essential for civic competence.

Methodology for Teaching Social Studies

Introduction

Historically, several influences played key roles in the shaping of the social studies curriculum. The nineteenth and the twentieth centuries have been dominated by traditional social studies curriculum focused on the mastery of low-level mental exercise questions that yield recitations of facts such as names of the rivers, capital cities, and important dates. The twenty-first century is marked with the emergence of new problems, values, and concerns that present new challenges to the social studies curriculum and teaching methodology.

In the twenty-first century, social studies method instruction should be consistent with the primary purpose of social studies; the methodology should challenge students with critical-thinking questions that require students to deeply think, analyze, synthesize, and evaluate questions, issues, and information in front of them. There is no one best, correct, right, or wrong answer in the social studies discussion classroom. Instead students should be empowered and encouraged to voice their views and perspectives on social issues, themes, and core democratic values, taking into consideration alternative views of the world from the lenses of the non-western populations.

At kindergarten, first grade, and second grade levels, you can introduce themes of social studies in developmental sequence. This means that instruction proceeds from the simple to the complex, from the familiar to the unfamiliar. For example, in lower elementary grade levels, students will be engaged in learning about concepts or information that is immediate and relevant to them. The focus should be more on helping them develop democratic dispositions.

Carol Seefeldt (1997) argued that to prepare children to become citizens of a democratic society children should be equipped with the knowledge, skills, and attitudes they need to participate in, and contribute to, the small democracies of their homes, their schools, immediate neighborhoods, as well as to become functioning citizens of the worldly society in the future. Children need to develop anticipatory, intuitive ideas and interests that will serve as a foundation for elaboration of the more complex understandings, attitudes, and skills in the intermediate grade (4–8) and upper grade (9–12) levels and as adults (Bredekamp and Rosegrant, 1995).

Questions Important to Social Studies Method Instruction

The Wh-questions—What and Why and How—are essential to an effective Social Studies Method instruction for the following reasons:

—What = Definition

Over the course of several semesters I have begun the first day of my class by asking students to write their definition of social studies before opening the book. The analysis of their written definitions reveals that one third of the class knows something about social studies, is already reading the book, and answering some questions. Another third wrote that history is social studies; and the last third are not sure exactly what social studies is. Their definitions were broader. With these misconceptions about the subject of social studies, it is critical to spend some time to review the definition of social studies in the early days of the class. Teachers equipped with an unambiguous and clear definition of the subject matter they are going to teach give students confidence because they see teachers as knowledgeable about what they are going to teach in K–12. Students come to my class unsure of what socials studies entails. At best they may have a broad definition of social studies. Most of them perceive social studies based on what and how they were taught. Mostly the teaching of social studies was reading a book and answering questions. For others history is equated to social studies. It is essential to help students learn about the nature and the purpose of social studies

—Why = Purpose Rationale, Motivation, and Interest

After developing familiarity with social studies, it important to understand and articulate its purpose—especially why it is being or should be taught. Unlike other subjects that are taught just for the grade and to prepare students to take high-stakes tests and move up to higher grade levels, the purpose of teaching social studies is beyond the grade. There is a much bigger purpose than just the grade. When method students are able to articulate a clear purpose behind teaching social studies, they can anticipate the methodology they will use to achieve that purpose.

—How = Instructional Methodology and Pedagogy

There is not one best instructional methodology to follow, because in any given lesson, the purpose should inform the appropriate methodology to use. Not the other way around. To maximize learning and achieve the purpose of social studies there are questions and suggestions for best practice in social studies that need to be taken into consideration in the process of planning and delivering a lesson.

When planning for social studies instruction, one needs to consider and find responses to questions at different stages of the planning process.

- Selection of materials—What teaching materials do I need for the targeted grade level?
- Why did I select this material, this book instead of that one?
- What content knowledge, skills, and dispositions are expected at this grade level?
- What lesson/unit format is appropriate for teaching this theme or lesson?
- Why do I use a unit format to teach rather than a single-lesson format?
- How many learning objectives do I need to achieve in this lesson?
- What activities are conducive to the mastery of content knowledge, skills, and development of dispositions?
- And how many activities are appropriate in 15-, 25-, 35-, or 45-minute lessons (the number of activities should match the number of learning objectives)?
- What questions do I need to ask to stimulate thoughtful responses from students?
- Why do I need to ask these questions?

Meaningful Connections

Students must be able to make connections of what they learn with what they have learned and what they are learning now and what they will learn in subsequent classes.

- Create and teach lessons that are practical and reflect life outside the classroom so students can connect and see how social studies concepts affect their lives and relate to their experiences.
- Incorporate knowledge and skills across academic areas (Math, Language Arts, Science, Current Events, etc.). After all, social studies themes are interrelated; it is only natural to teach social studies using an integrated instructional approach (unit plan rather than a single-lesson plan approach). The integrated approach helps students see things from multiple perspectives and the interconnections among subjects, people, environment, food, transportation, music, etc.
- Foster in-depth thinking and meaningful understanding of facts through few topics. To achieve this you need to spend a reasonable amount of time with few topics to enhance deep learning and critical thinking rather than covering several topics using an overview approach. At best, students gain a shallow knowledge of the concept being introduced; at worst, they do not remember anything about the topic.

Core Democratic Values

What are they and why are they important? The more people know the core democratic values it is likely that they will be committed and try to live up to these values. Teachers should therefore help students understand the value of and analyze the issues that can arise when the value guides behavior. As students discuss and debate socially sensitive issues, they will make their arguments and decisions on the basis of those core democratic values (Ochoa, 1988).

- Make core democratic values the basis of your social studies instruction.
- Engage students in discussions that challenge their prior beliefs, biases, and stereotypical mindsets about social phenomena.
- Encourage cooperative learning, role playing, problem solving, discussions, debates, factual reasoning, and arguments.
- Remind students why it is critical to develop critical-thinking dispositions and grow into informed decision-making citizens.

Challenging Activities

- Engage students in open-ended activities to stimulate their creativity and imagination in the process of completing the activities.
- Ask WH-questions that require explanation, clarification, and elaboration more than just yes/no answers from students.
- Remind students there are no right or wrong answers during discussions of social issues.
- Well-articulated arguments supported by facts and drawn from multiple perspectives are the hallmarks of learning in social studies.

Less is more.

Assigning more homework does not challenge students—it simply gives them more to do and less time to think critically about what they're doing.

- Engage your students in deep thinking about a few things by not having them think superficially about many things.

Active Learning vs. Passive Learning

- Students learn more by doing and less by listening passively.
- Engage students in activities that allow them to manipulate ideas, materials, and practice life skills that prepare them for active participation in public service in their community.
- Engage students in group inquiry and research projects in and beyond the classroom.
- Students should be given the open choice and flexibility to complete projects beyond the confines of the classroom.

Assessment vs. Evaluation in Social Studies

Assessing is checking the progress of learning during a given lesson. It is embedded in the lesson as it evolves and does not require a grade. Feedback is needed here but in the form of positive reinforcement so students develop a sense of accomplishment.

- Develop assessment in social studies to value students' thinking and their growth into becoming informed citizens rather than results in standardized test scores.
- Develop authentic forms of assessment to equip students with social skills essential in real-life situations.

Allow and encourage non-written presentation of information such as charts, tables, and graphs.

Evaluating is judging the quality of the work produced by students at a given time period against a set of learning-expectation criteria. The judgment is sanctioned with a number in percentage, points, or a letter.

Grade-Level Learning Expectations

The learning expectations provide illustrations of the purposes, knowledge, skills, and democratic dispositions (values and attitudes) that students should master by the completion of a lesson.

Learner Expectations for History

- The study of history allows students to understand their place in time and location.
- Historical thinking skills enable learners to evaluate evidence, develop comparative and causal analyses, interpret the historical record, and construct historical arguments and perspectives to make informed decisions in current social realities.

Learning Expectations for Geography

- The study of geography enables students to develop an understanding of the special contexts of people, places, and environments.
- It provides knowledge of the Earth's physical and human systems and interdependency of living things and physical environments.
- It enables students to understand and make informed decisions about local and global issues.

Learning Expectations for Civics

- The study of civics and government is to prepare citizens for informed decision-making for common good.
- Develops dispositions or characters that enhance the individual capacity to participate in the political process and contribute to the healthy functioning of the political system and improvement of society.

Social Studies Themes Are Interrelated

Very rarely some themes may dominate one lesson more than others, but in general all themes are highly interrelated. For example, to understand the theme of culture, students need to know and understand the theme of time continuity and change, the relationships between people, places, and environments, and the role of civic ideals and practices. Likewise to understand the theme of power, authority, and governance, students must understand different cultures, the relationships between people, places, and environments, and the interconnections among individuals, groups, and institutions. It is important to keep in mind that history and geography cut across all the themes because historical knowledge contributes to the understanding of all the other themes.

Learning Expectations for Culture

Purpose: Cultural understanding helps students make informed decisions in an increasingly inter-dependent and interconnected world.

Questions to Explore at K–5 Grade Level

- What is culture?
- How are people alike and different?
- What causes cultural changes?
- What does it mean to be a minority?
- How does diversity affect culture?

Learning Expectation for Time, Continuity, and Change

Purpose: Students will gain an understating of how important historical events have shaped and changed today's world.

Questions to Explore at K–5 Grade Level

- How do we know about the past?
- Why do we learn about the past?
- How were things in the past?
- How are they different from today?

Learning Expectations for Production, Distribution, and Consumption

Purpose: Students will gain a better understanding of the global economic decisions that affect their daily lives.

Questions to Explore at K–5 Grade Level

- What is the difference between wants and needs?
- Can we have everything we want?
- Can we have everything we need?
- What choices do we have to make in times of scarcity?
- How does affluence affect individual economic decisions?
- How do we get our goods and services?

Learning Expectations for Global Connections

Purpose: Students will gain a better understanding of the increasingly complex connections among individuals and nations in order to make informed decisions about different types of global connections (social, economic, cultural, and environmental).

Questions to Explore at K–5 Grade Level

- What is global interdependence?
- Give three examples of global interdependence
- How does global interdependence affect your community?
- What does it mean to go global?
- What are long-term consequences of globalization?

Learning Expectations for Science, Technology, and Society

Purpose: An understanding of science and technology enables students to question and analyze the impact of science and technology on today's society.

Questions to Explore at K–5 Grade Level

- What has led to the advances of science and technology throughout history?
- How did science change people's lives?
- What are the limitations of science and technology today?
- How should technology be used for common good?

Writing Learning Objectives

Focus on Three Areas of Learning: Cognitive, Psychomotor, and Democratic Dispositions

Traditionally, behavioral learning objectives are stated in a lesson plan focusing on knowledge and skills. The goal is to be able to assess what students will know and be able to do with the information delivered in the lesson. For example, learning objectives are usually stated in a specific language with action verbs that describe activities that can be observed and easy to assess or evaluate. Most people have used "understand" as a learning objective. Even though to "understand" also means to know, operationally it is not observable. How do you know students understand? How do you assess understanding? How much is understood in a lesson? We can always assume that students understand what we are teaching only if they are able to behave in a way that is expected of them in the lesson (doing and behavior are observable). Then we can be assured that they understand meaning and that they know and can do whatever is expected of them in the lesson. A typical statement of learning objectives with action verbs is in reference to what students are able to do at the end of the 34–45 minutes of instruction.

1. Describe perspectives that currently define social studies.
2. Master social studies instructional planning skills such as lessons and integrated unit planning.
3. Identify and describe the four multicultural perspectives and incorporate them in social studies curriculum.
4. Discuss the fundamental reasons cooperative learning is a powerful instructional tool for teaching social studies.
5. Plan social studies instruction using research or inquiry-based strategies.
6. Discuss the rationale behind teaching citizenship as the primary goal of social studies.
7. Identify and use GLCEs and guidelines for teaching history with primary sources, conducting a historical inquiry, historical fiction, and timelines.
8. Identify and use GLCEs and guidelines for teaching geographic concepts to young children.
9. Discuss the fundamental reasons for making global connections, interdependence, and current events part of social studies instruction.
10. Identify and use GLCEs and guidelines for teaching economic concepts to young children.

One of the fundamental goals of social studies education in the twenty-first century is to prepare students to become citizens who would make informed decisions to serve the common good. To achieve this goal a number of needs must be fulfilled. Subject area associations and states have established content standards to specify what students should know and be able to do in various subjects during the K–12 school years. The standards are intended to focus on teaching and learning and provide a basis for accountability:

- Standards are stated in ways that make them difficult to address. Some standards are too vast (example) to provide goals with adequate clarity and guidance to instruction and assessment.
- Different teachers in good faith emphasize different aspects of the content.
- Some standards are too short.
- The focus is too specific and arbitrary.
- The situation is far more complicated by textbooks.
- The adoption of textbooks that include as many standards and benchmarks as possible.

By the end of the lesson students will be able to:

- Describe ...
- Know ...
- Compare ...
- List ...
- Organize ...
- Draw ...
- Write ...
- Etc.

When learning objectives are stated using action verbs, it is important to develop activities that students are engaged in to reflect the objectives. With two objectives stated, prepare two activities. With three objectives, prepare three activities and teach to the stated objectives.

Essential Learning in Social Studies

In social studies instruction, the essence of learning goes beyond cognitive learning and psycho-motor learning. The democratic dispositions are the added dimension that is critical because it is the essence of social studies instruction. We expect students to know (knowledge), to do (skills), but also to develop dispositions that prepare them for developing civic competence, and to become open minded, tolerant, and informed decision makers for the common good.

In social studies instruction, learning objectives or outcomes in a lesson plan should include knowledge, skills, and democratic dispositions. Table 1 is a good illustration of the areas of learning that are essential in social studies instruction.

Table 1. Essence of Student Learning (Knowledge) Cognitive Skills (Psychomotor) and Behavior (Dispositions)

(Cognitive) Knowledge	(Psychomotor) Skills	(Dispositions) Values
Knowledge is cognitive—It is about understanding concepts, theories, philosophies, concepts, formulas, etc.	Skills are observable, action related; they are demonstrated by doing, acting, creating. They are a visible and concrete application of knowledge.	Values are constructs—They are behavioral or attitudinal. They are demonstrated through feelings, emotions, passion, sensitivity, remorse.
Knowledge outcomes	Skill outcomes—Writing, explaining, analyzing, synthesizing, interviewing, problem solving, speaking	Values outcomes—Showing open-mindedness about different values, perspectives, and beliefs; engaging in social action for social justice and common good.

Cognitive Learning

Examples of contexts for capturing the essence of student learning at the cognitive level.

Students are engaged in the discussion of the core democratic values.

Knowledge and Information about:
- Core democratic values.
- The world, its geography, people, cultures.
- The history, settlement, growth, and development of the United States.
- The neighborhood, community, home state; how people live and work there; how they meet their basic needs of life; how they interact and depend on each other.
- The legal and political system of the local community, the state, and the nation.
- The world of work and orientation to various careers.
- Basic human institutions, such as the family.
- How people use and misuse natural resources.
- The problems and challenges that confront people today in the realm of social living and human relations in the local, state, national, and international arenas.
- The basic social functions that characterize all societies such as producing, transporting, distributing, and consuming goods and services; providing for education, recreation, and government; protecting and conserving human and natural resources; expressing esthetic and religious drives; communicating with others.

Psychomotor Learning

Example of contexts for capturing the essence of student learning at the psychomotor level.

Students are engaged in the discussion and execution of tasks of the core democratic values.

Develop Social Skills
- Live and work together; take turns; respect the rights of others; be socially sensitive.
- Learn self-control and self-direction.
- Share ideas and experiences with others

Develop Study Skills and Work Habits
- Use maps, globes, charts, graphs, graphic and pictorial materials.
- Locate and gather information from a variety of sources.
- Write and read reports, make public speeches, listen when others are reporting.
- Read social studies materials for diverse purposes.
- Organize information into usable structures such as outlines, charts, and time lines; classify and sequence; take notes, keep records, write summaries.
- Conduct inquiry on a problem of interest.

Develop Group Work Skills
- Work cooperatively in groups and on committees and assume various roles in small groups such as chair person, secretary, or committee member.
- Participate in group discussion; lead a discussion.
- Participate in group decision making.

Develop Intellectual Skills
- Define and identify problems; relate prior experience to present inquiry.
- Form and test hypotheses; draw conclusion based on information.
- Analyze and synthesize data.
- Think critically; distinguish between fact and opinion. Learn to separate relevant from irrelevant information; recognize bias in persuasive materials such as advertising, political statements, and propaganda.
- Sense cause and effect relationships.
- Compare differing points of view.

Much of social studies teaching is directed toward the achievement of more than one objective at the same time.

Disposition Development
- Show examples of contexts for capturing the essence of student learning at affective level. Students are engaged in the discussion of the core democratic values.

Develop Attitude and Value
- Be able to make decisions that involve choices between competing values.

- Develop a reasoned loyalty to this country.
- Develop a sense of respect for the ideals, heritages, and institutions of this nation.
- Develop a feeling of kinship toward human beings everywhere.

Critical Thinking–Based Teaching and Learning: An Effective Model for Social Studies Method Instruction

Based on my teaching experiences overall, one of the challenges faced by faculty in charge of Social Studies Method instruction is how to consistently engage students in discussions of topics or issues that equip them with critical-thinking skills. Discussions that have a clear purpose yield thought provoking and insightful feedback from students. As an approach to help students develop critical-thinking skills and grow as critical-thinking citizens, Critical Thinking–Based Teaching and Learning is based on using topics, cooperative/collaborative inquiry, and reflection as teaching and learning tools. Students' reports and reflections on the projects suggest that (1) more students are actively engaged in their learning, (2) student–student interaction is enhanced, (3) students make connections of the concepts learned with current events and realities in the community, and (4) students' ability to reflect and think critically is stimulated.

One of the fundamental goals of social studies education in the twenty-first century is to prepare students for becoming citizens who will make informed decisions to serve common good.

Engage Students in Social Action

The professional literature in multicultural education (Banks, 2003) advocated for the integration of multicultural perspectives into social studies. These perspectives include four approaches to integration.

The contribution approach is an effort on the part of teachers to commit one day in their schedule to celebrate historical heroes from underrepresented or minority groups. The criticism leveled against this approach is that it is lacking in-depth learning. Another approach that is similar to the contribution approach is the additive approach. As its name suggests, it is an approach where one aspect of history or historical experience lived by minorities is added to what is considered essential content curriculum. Teachers are not under any pressure to implement the added historical piece, especially when it is construed as "an added" it is not implemented consistently. A teacher may choose to teach about the civil rights movement only if it is part of state-mandated content at a given grade level. A third approach is referred to as transformation approach; teachers select multiple teaching materials to teach one concept in order for students to learn different perspectives about the concept. For example, teaching Christopher Columbus Day from a European American perspective only as a celebration is promoting European cultural hegemony. However, teaching it in contrast with a Native American perspective as a form of oppression gives students another perspective on Christopher Columbus Day. Teaching is conducted with the goal to transform students to develop open-mindedness and democratic dispositions, such as developing sensitivity to other cultures, equality, pursuit of happiness, and justice. A classroom where students are engaged in discussions and activities that foster the transformation approach, are those students who transform intellectually from being narrow-minded citizens who hold on to the status quo to being open-minded citizens who aspire for change.

Finally, the social action approach empowers and expects students to take action. The action is usually a service-learning project.

Social action is therefore a continuum of possible activities ranging from single efforts requiring small commitments of time and talent to long-term projects requiring a regular commitment of time and multiple intellectual and social skills. These activities can involve regularly picking up litter, reading stories to children in younger grades during rainy lunch times, making Valentine's Day cards for nursing home residents, washing dishes at a soup kitchen for homeless people, or working to have a stop sign installed at a busy intersection where school children cross. Prior to engaging in those activities, students must be made aware of the project and understand the rationale for doing it.

Management of Learning in a
Social Studies Classroom

Introduction

Volumes have been written about classroom management and yet, it continues to be a timeless topic of wide interest and concern for teachers and school administrators. Butchart (1998) suggested that classroom management needs to move beyond the current tendency to rely on a checklist of quick fixes and engage in more ethical foundations of classroom management. Classroom management is not a simple matter of one technique versus another. Through classroom discipline, teachers enact social and moral relationships with the learners. Currently, the modes of classroom management in use in most classrooms are derived from behaviorist dogma. For example, discipline is managed through threats or rewards. Teachers gain student compliance through this practice, but they subvert the intellectual growth of the learner. In "Classroom Management Strategies: Gaining and Maintaining Students' Cooperation," Cangelosi (2000) presented a model for classroom management that helps to gain and maintain students' cooperation. The Teaching Process Model is composed of six stages: (1) determine needs of students, (2) determine learning goals, (3) design learning activities, (4) prepare for the learning activities, (5) conduct the learning activities, and (6) determine how well students have achieved the learning goal. Manke (1997) suggested that classroom management and beliefs about teaching and learning are a seamless whole that contribute to the same teaching agenda. Teachers are urged to evaluate their efforts to control student behavior in terms of whether or not those efforts are promoting student learning. To separate these two elements is to lose sight of the fact that education is about learning, not about behavior control. Marzano (2003) defined classroom management as the "confluence of teacher actions in four distinct areas: (1) establishing and enforcing rules and procedures, (2) carrying out disciplinary actions, (3) maintaining effective teacher and student relationships, and (4) maintaining an appropriate mental set for management" (p. 88). An analysis of these four areas of concern in the process of classroom management evokes a powerful insight in effective classroom management. Marzano claimed that only when effective practices in these four areas are employed and working in concert is a classroom effectively managed. His emphasis on the word "effective" implies a commitment to thinking through each identified area before taking action.

Traynor (2002) studied and evaluated five discipline management strategies for pedagogical soundness: (1) coercive, (2) laissez-faire, (3) task oriented, (4) authoritative, and (5) intrinsic. While his study found the authoritative and intrinsic strategies the most effective, he concluded little is known about what contributes to a teacher's choice of one of these classroom strategies. Traynor (2003) further found that teacher conviction of the instructional dependability of these strategies and the expectations of teachers regarding (1) rewards from the teaching experience, (2) who is responsible for student discipline, and (3) student behavior, contribute to teachers selecting any one of these strategies to guide classroom discipline practices. Johnson (1994) presented the challenges faced by novice teachers in their efforts to find a balance between caring and discipline. Rimm-Kaufman, La Paro, Downer, and Pianta (2005) contended that in classrooms with high-quality teacher-learner interactions, a teacher shows sensitivity to learners' academic needs, and readily modifies lessons and learning activities to fit the cognitive maturity of the learners. Jean Pierre's (2004) study found the quality of instruction is central to the interplay between students' interactions and teachers' classroom management practices. Arends (2001) suggested that the causes of misbehavior are due to boring classroom activities, authoritarian dispositions that prevail in schools, and the need for attention children miss at home. While educators might subscribe to the above-mentioned models on classroom management, these studies seldom mention reflection as a key element of the management process in classrooms of the twenty-first century.

For more than a decade, I assumed supervisory roles in classroom settings at kindergarten, elementary, middle, and secondary school levels to observe teachers during their probationary years to prepare them for tenure, and student-teachers during their internships to prepare them for their teaching licensure. This has helped me to better understand and describe management styles that are often used in the classrooms. Teachers who construe classroom management as a set of rules without any prior reflection on personal philosophy, values, and developmental appropriateness of the rules are likely to face resistance and chaos in their classroom.

The term "reflection" is a blending of both thought and action in such a way that they are enriched and supported by one another. Some definitions of reflective practice highlight its most salient characteristics. Consider for example Dewey's (1933) definition of reflective thinking as the "active, persistent and careful consideration of any belief or supposed form of knowledge in light of the grounds that support it" (p. 9). Schon (1987) concurs with Dewey's emphasis on action as an essential aspect of the reflective process. He defines the reflective practitioner as one who engages in reflection-in-action and interior observation and criticism of personal actions. Reflection calls for the ability to think on one's feet during the orchestration of lessons in the classroom. We plan and try out new actions, test our tentative understanding of them, or affirm the moves we have taken to change things for the better. Schon suggested that reflectivity in teaching leads to creativity, a special type of competence some teachers show when faced with ambiguous or conflicting situations. He believes reflective teachers respond to these situations by asking questions such as "What are my students experiencing?" and "What can I do to improve?" There are several contemporary proponents of reflective classroom management (Charles, 2002; Charles and Senter, 2002; Evertson, Emmer, and Worshan, 2003; Gartrell, 2003; Kauffman, Mostert, Trent, and Hallahan, 2002; Woody, 2001). Woody (2001) suggested that a reflective approach depends on the teacher's ability to function in perceptive, creative ways. A reflective attitude requires teachers to examine what they are doing in order to discover ways to improve. Kauffmann et al. (2002) provided the following questions for reflection:

- Could this problem be a result of in appropriate curriculum or teaching strategies?
- What do I demand and prohibit?
- Which certain behaviors bother me and what should I do about them? (pp. 5 – 11).
- Is this behavior developmentally significant?

Dinkelman (2003) asserted that reflective teaching is self-study of teaching and learning experiences and behaviors. By self-study, Dinkelman meant "intentional and systematic inquiry into one's own practice" (p. 3). It is important for teachers to find time to think about what is being taught and its impact on classroom management. Loughran (2002) viewed reflection as a meaningful way of approaching learning about teaching. Reflection construed as such, places an emphasis on learning through questioning for understanding. Ross (2002) described reflective teaching practices in the following manner:

> Examining teaching practice through a reflective lens has gained acceptance in the last decade in teacher education and beginning teacher induction programs. The implementation, however, can be very different from the theory. Reflection is not a skill most teachers bring with them when they begin the profession; in fact many highly experienced teachers are novices at reflective practice. Initial attempts at reflection are generally little more than descriptions of classroom practice. For most teachers, moving beyond descriptive thought and writing requires training and a supportive environment. (p. 12)

Henderson (1992) described reflective practice as a model of inquiry, where the teacher seeks opportunities for dialogue with students and engages in self-examination. He further suggested that the key elements of a reflective teacher are an ethic of caring, a constructivist approach to teaching, and artistic problem solving.

With increasing diverse classroom demographics, alternative management strategies are needed to meet the unpredictable behavior problems that may occur in today's classrooms. According to Wentz (2001), no behavior management model is 100 percent effective for every teacher and every student; therefore, to resort to using a control-management approach as the only solution is precarious. Teaching in classrooms with a diverse group of students has no fixed answers. Rather, reflective thinking and decision-making are models that can be applied to many different situations (Kauffman et al. 2002). However, when looking into classrooms, I am finding reflection a missing element in the management process of pre-service teachers and teachers new to the classroom, in particular. Some tend to blindly adopt new classroom-management fads without questioning their value. It is common for inexperienced teachers to focus more on classroom management, lesson delivery, and daily survival over reflection. I have heard comments such as: "I've got enough to think about right now." "I do not have time for this." "The lesson went well." In fact, implementation of tips and checklists without reflection is not necessarily conducive to effective classroom management. I agree with Schulman (1988) that reflection is what a teacher does when he or she stops to contemplate the teaching and learning that transpired. Kauffman et al. (2002) explained the importance of doing so.

> First impressions about a problem can be misleading. Our experiences in classrooms with children and youth lead us to believe that even outstanding teachers sometimes jump to conclusions about what the problem is rather than taking a more reflective, analytic approach to identifying it. As a consequence of not being sufficiently reflective and analytical, a teacher can waste a lot of time and energy dealing with an issue that is not the most important while neglecting a more significant problem (p. 3).

When teachers engage in models based on systematic inquiry or reflection, they gain more insight into their own beliefs and actions. For example, Peters' (1991) model, known as "DATA: Describe Analyze, Theorize, and Act," guides teachers to examine their own practices by describing a classroom event, analyzing the event, developing a theory, and acting. Eby (1997) introduced "Reflective Action," a model with a list of questions about teachers' reflective actions.

The POC Model

I designed and implemented the POC Model in 2000 with pre-service and first- and second-year classroom teachers. POC stands for three areas of reflection: knowledge of self, awareness and knowledge of students, and curriculum planning and implementation. The model uses guiding questions to help the teacher's reflection upon the three areas. The questions in POC are similar to those in Eby's (1977) model, but are related more to self-knowing, knowing of students, and the curriculum. I have shared this reflective-management process with approximately 160 K–12 pre-service and first- and second-year classroom teachers. They were asked to use journals to record their reflections over a three-month time period. Feedback about the use of POC was positive. While it was time consuming, teachers obtained useful information they could use as they created their reflective classroom-management system. The pre-service teachers adjusted their lessons to include less lecturing and paper-and-pencil assignments. First- and second-year teachers were able to adjust their lessons to include more activities such as role-playing and inquiry projects.

Knowing of Self

Machado and Botnarescue (2001) observed that self-knowledge should precede any attempt to engage in some instructional interaction with students. The instructional material or methods a teacher uses need to be based on his or her educational philosophy. It is important that the teacher be guided in her/his choice of learning materials by her/his philosophy of teaching. Consistency between educational philosophy and practice is essential in the process of reflective classroom management. Knowing yourself and your values are critical elements of the reflective management process. There is much to be gained in maintaining consistency between one's philosophy, values, and practices. Another advantage in being consistent is that it has a positive impact on teachers' commitment.

Knowing Your Students

Cangelosi (2000) acknowledges that knowing students and being aware of their individual differences in assigning learning tasks is essential. Wentz (2001) asserts that a teacher's attitude in the classroom is also important in managing student behaviors. A positive attitude is reflected in a teacher's enthusiasm and commitment to the students. Students are usually quick to sense a teacher's stamina and decide whether they should cooperate or not. I concur with these views and add that the reflective management practices bear on the quality of the rapport teachers have established with students, rather than on a set of authoritarian rules that they have established. Allowing oneself time outside the teaching period gives a teacher an opportunity to construct a detailed lesson; introduce it in a sequence that takes into account the cognitive, physical, emotional ability and educational needs of the students in the classroom; and bring it to closure before the end of the class period. It is important to place students first, by responding to their immediate needs in the classroom and moving on. When teachers take time to address unrelated issues that seem to be emotionally critical to students, they are more likely to run into fewer discipline problems, capture students' interest in the lesson, and gain the time wasted. Positive relationships with students help improve classroom management. Reflective teachers have good relationships with their students. Good relationships not only lay the groundwork for students' learning, but they are also the keystones of reflective classroom management. Classroom discussions sail smoothly when the teacher knows individual student characteristics in the classroom and connects the curricular content to their experiences beyond the classroom. For example, if the teacher is aware of a student's learning difficulties, or home life, or hobby, it makes all the difference in the relationship between the teacher and the student.

When mentoring classroom teachers, I encourage them to reflect upon their experiences by answering questions related to the curriculum: the planning stage and the implementation stage. In the planning stage, it is critical to think about the relationship you would like to have with your students and the purpose of the lesson you plan to teach. I also ask teachers to answer questions about the instructional materials for the lesson. Each choice teachers make in terms of learning materials is another aspect of classroom management. Answers to these questions will help guide decision-making prior to teaching.

Reflective teachers do not rely solely on commercially prepared lesson plans and curricular materials when they search for new knowledge and strategies to use in their classrooms. Instead they invent their own strategies and create their own materials through research efforts and involve students in the process of learning in different ways. This helps to keep them on task and reduce opportunities for behavioral problems. The planning stage should be based on the knowledge that every student learns at a different pace, therefore the instruction needs to be flexible and the teacher needs to be ready to make adjustments when she or he senses that students are not getting it, or as they come to stumbling blocks in the lesson.

There is no doubt teachers are actively involved in decision making, acting, doing, and behaving in different ways every second of a school day. In the process, van Manen (1990) suggested that a teacher's ability to make thoughtful classroom decisions that affect students positively must be guided by pedagogical standards. These standards require that teachers engage in a reflective process that never stops when the process ends. For example, in the teaching process, a teacher does not stop reflecting at the closure of a lesson; instead she or he reflects actively about what has transpired in the lesson in order to recapture the nature of the classroom events such as: Teacher–student interactions, student–student interactions, questioning techniques, responses to questions, and the general mood of the class. Reflection needs to be consistent with personal philosophy, beliefs, and values as a basis for action, with the intent to improve one's own classroom performance and students' learning.

Where the students sit in a classroom can have an impact on their attitude to each other and the teacher, the teacher's attitude toward them, how they interact, and the type of tasks they can perform. It is not always good to have students who are buddies or related in a certain way to sit together. Very often the types of chairs, tables, or desks in the classroom may restrict the teacher. Usually they are fixed or too heavy to move. Classroom furniture can affect the learning ambiance but the choice is beyond the control of the teacher most of the time. However, when the chairs are freestanding, the teacher should make good use of the opportunity. For example, activities where the teacher needs to teach from the front, a horseshoe arrangement will be necessary because it allows easy, face-to-face contact between the students and between the teacher and the students. During an open-pair work activity dominated by a verbal interaction between two students across the classroom under the teacher's supervision, there is no need to arrange the seats in any certain way. In group work, the seating arrangement is always dictated by the size of the class, the size of the group, the types of activities, and the type of furniture in the classroom. For an activity that involves a lot of reading and writing, the teacher would consider turning students away from each other to give them the freedom to concentrate.

Be aware of slow and fast learners and also the home background and prior knowledge of your students in relation to the material you are about to introduce. When the material to learn is new, children as well as young adults need more time to reflect or think about what it is they are learning. Some students will quickly master the material while others will need more time and further explanation of the material. Do not focus too much on individual problems when you have the attention of the whole class. Deal with them during breaks or group work. The focus in reflective management is on using reflective practices to anticipate and prevent undesired behavior, or prevent chaos before it takes place. It also will help you in managing your time during the lesson-implementation phase.

When teachers engage in this process of questioning, as outlined in Figures 1 and 2, they begin to clarify their philosophy of teaching and develop their own ethics of caring and decision-making in the best interest of learners in the classroom. Additionally, during the delivery or implementation of the lesson, the teacher is prompted to keep foremost in mind considerations about self and students. In addition, time management and assessment of the teaching and learning process should be considered. Questions for reflection in these areas are listed under the Implementation Stage.

Classroom Management Tips

Self-Management Strategies
- Establish rapport with students (know your students' names as early and quickly as possible, know their hobbies, what makes them smile, and what make them sad).
- Define and clarify rules and expectations (involve them in making rules and expectations in the classroom).
- Make sure expectations are clearly visible (write in bold, color).
- Authoritative not authoritarian (voice projection, firm but fair, tough love).
- Show enthusiasm (smile, show humor, be natural, know your content and love it).
- Dress professionally (not jeans, not too tight, not too loose, not provocative, not dull—just be elegant and professionally attractive).
- A model for good citizenry (volunteerism, sharing, caring).

Space-Management Strategies
- Seating arrangement (rows, groups, semi-circle, horseshoe, circle, assigned, student related).
- Be aware of the group dynamics (identify cliques, sense of community).
- Make room for late students (back seats, provide written instructions).
- Provide developmentally-appropriate learning activities for students.
- Be able to distinguish students' needs and wants (clear traffic areas).
- Materials (supplies, books, handouts, pencils, use of pencil sharpener).
- Bulletin board (purposeful and attractive).
- Music (songs, music).

Curriculum-Management Strategies
- Understand the school culture (federal, state, district, school, community expectations in terms of knowledge, curriculum, hygiene, code of conduct).
- Establish rapport with students (know students beyond their names, communicate with parents via letter, email, telephone, at-home visits, invitation to the rooms).
- Define and clarify rules and expectations (make grading rubric available for students, be consistent but flexible).
- Reach a consensus with students (communicate your expectations, listen to student suggestions).
- Share responsibilities (with students, between students, shift delegation of power).
- Use of the blackboard (flipchart, overhead, PowerPoint, TV, audio).
- Write detailed lesson plans (include purpose/rationale, time for each activity; be consistent and clear; set realistic objectives and teach to those objectives only).
- Avoid careless mistakes (spelling).
- Remember students' different approaches to learning (visual, auditory, kinesthetic, versatile)
- Survive only as entertainer (make learning fun).
- Maintain eye contact with all students (move, be aware of the seating arrangement in your room, use proximity).
- Involve all students (use what you know about their individual interest, social life, and life and integrate that in your lesson).

- Listen and give positive reinforcement (give meaningful, relevant reinforcements).
- Capture all students' attention when you talk (you can be silent for a while, wait, and call on those who do not follow).

Instructional Decisions

- Brainstorming (put students in the mood for learning, check prior knowledge, and begin your lesson from where students are). Clarify objectives of the lesson and connect with real-life examples.
- Master the material (know your content but listen to your students; teach from the known to the unknown).
- Clarify the purpose of the activity (help students see the meaning of the lesson in real life and make connections with their own experiences).
- Delivery speed (speak in developmentally appropriate speed, pause, rephrase, use examples, draw, act, use students as examples).
- Planning (always plan ahead of time, use different resources, find sounding boards to review your lesson plans).
- Be prepared (never assume anything about anything).
- Make good use of breaks (shadow on each student to get to know him/her better to make a difference in his/her life).
- Remember students' time limitations (use wait time effectively and consistently).
- Model (after modeling give students ample opportunities to practice).
- Assess the learning (show evidence of learning that takes place; if learning did not take place, be prepared to reflect your plan of improvement for the subsequent lesson).
- Teacher-talking time versus student-talking time (balance your talking time with that of students by involving more students in the learning activities.
- Be creative (initiate learning activities that are reasonably challenging and meaningful to students).

Dealing with Behavior Issues

- Be alert (think on your feet, anticipate disruptive behaviors).
- Do not use threats (never threaten to punish unless you have the power to do so).
- Try to understand your students through communication.
- Be open to communication (devote some time [five minutes] each day for each student for a one-on-one informal communication).
- Make room for choices (value alternative ideas from students).
- Be aware that students expect you to be predictable; do not expect them to be predictable, at least at the elementary level.
- Do not take students' outbursts personally (once in a while let children be children).
- Sometimes you need to teach children something other than content (notice when students are not ready to learn and are rather interested in something else; honor their interest through negotiation).

- Think of the student, not the content (when the student is happy, the learning is natural).
- Avoid learning through coercion and bribes (use dialogue and common sense).

Guiding Questions for Self-Knowing and Knowing Learners

Self-Knowledge
- What do I believe my students need to succeed in school and life?
- What is my belief in how children learn?
- What is my role?

Knowing Learners
- Who are my students?
- Where do they live?
- Who are their parents?
- What are their needs (i.e., food, clothing, shelter, nurturing)?
- In what way will they learn this material best?

Guiding Questions for Lesson Planning and Implementation of Lessons

- Why did I select this topic?
- Did I choose a diversity of materials and methods?
- What knowledge did I expect students to gain from the lesson?
- What skills do I expect them to develop?
- What values do I expect them to learn and what activities will they be engaged in?
- What information do I need?
- Where can I get it?
- Where I locate the instructional resources on this topic?
- How do I change the seating arrangement to fit the activity at hand? Why?
- How are my teaching strategies related to the seating pattern? Why?

Implementation Stage: The Lesson
- Is my questioning clear enough?
- Am I using developmentally appropriate language in my questioning?
- Do I ask comprehension questions?
- Are my questions clear and specific?
- Do I observe a wait time for students?
- Do I ask the same students?
- Why are students showing this behavior?
- Did I do that right?
- How are students experiencing this material?
- How do I know learning has transpired?
- What is the best way to find out?
- Is it the only way to assess learning?

- How much time will be needed to complete this activity?
- Do I have time for slow learners?
- How do I keep fast learners on task?
- How many activities do students need to complete?

Reflective classroom management is a process designed to create a proactive classroom environment that will allow teachers to spend a considerable amount of classroom time in instructional activities, thus resulting in increased student learning.

Reflective teachers are sensitive to subtle cues from students about what is happening in the classroom (Kounin, 1977). Their insight helps them reflect upon potential problems and take action in time to prevent conflicts from occurring.

It is essential to consider reflection a constant and critical check on personal beliefs in relation to student characteristics in the teaching and learning process. Students will develop confidence and enhance their decision-making skills through reflective practice.

Social studies teachers travel with students though time and space exploring the wonders of humanity. Students have memories of activities and projects in which they took part in elementary school such as The Boston Tea Party, dramatizing Harriet Tubman's role in the Underground Railroad, inviting families to the school's international festivals, or constructing maps. Other memories include reading from textbooks and answering questions at the end of the chapter, and memorizing lists of names, dates, and places. The distinction between positive and negative experiences is the level of students' engagement. The positive memories were the ones in which students were actively involved in the learning sequence.

Characteristics of a Meaningful Social Studies Instruction

The subject matter is drawn from history, geography, and a broad range of social sciences, and from the experiences of children.

A global perspective is apparent throughout, with attention to non-western, non-Christian cultures as well as those of the west.

The organizational format is interdisciplinary study around some topic of interest.

Social studies experiences can help children understand and appreciate the various lifestyles of the human race through direct contact with artifacts and people from cultures other than their own. Resources needed to provide such experiences are not available in most American communities.

This template is intended to help methods instructors and students. It provides a collection of topics that students are encouraged to read and respond to in writing. Questions have been developed to accompany the module and are both related to these topics and may be used together with the assignment template. The questions are intended to encourage discussion among students.

Pre-Reading Activity

(To be assigned after the first meeting and use Form A.)

Pre-reading Assignment Reflection and Response Form

Student teachers will use this form to respond in writing, following the reading of the chosen topic. Topics for reading will be chosen on the basis of the management needs expressed by individual students.

Introductory Questions/Activity

The first day of seminar is appropriate to introduce the module to students. At the start of Part 3, have one or two questions for student teachers to focus on one of the related classroom-management topics in the template. For example, you can introduce classroom management as the first category among the six categories listed in the template.

Classroom Management

Introductory Questions/Activity

- What comes to mind when you think of the term "classroom management"?
- Why does classroom management matter?
- What do you want to know about classroom management?
- What is your greatest fear, if any, about classroom management?

Have students respond to each of the questions in writing. Have them form groups of three or four based on the grade levels, and have them share their responses in their respective groups. Then have each group select a member of its group to read the group's response to the whole class. Or you can choose to have student-teachers share their writings in class by reflecting aloud. The purpose of this activity is to stimulate discussion on the topic.

Follow-up Questions/Activity

In light of the reading and discussions in class, the instructor will ask students to respond in writing to the following:

- Write an outline of a lesson using the insights gained from your reading and the discussions.
- Identify and list a few essential management strategies that will help you deliver better lessons to maximize learning.

Personal Qualities

Introductory Questions/Activities

- What specific personal qualities should teachers have?
- Why do personal qualities matter?
- What personal qualities do you have?
- Why is knowing your personal qualities important?

Have students respond to each of the questions in writing. Have them form groups of three or four based on the grade levels, and have them share their responses in their respective groups. Then have each group select a member of its group to read the group's response to the whole class. Or you can choose to have individual students share his or her writings in class by reflecting aloud. The purpose of this activity is to stimulate discussion on the topic.

Follow-up Questions/Activity

In light of the reading and discussions, the instructor will ask students to respond in writing to the following:

- Write an outline of a lesson using the insights gained from your reading and the discussions.
- List a few essential management strategies that will help you deliver better lessons to maximize learning.

Introductory Questions/Activity

- Why is physical arrangement important?
- List some seating arrangements and discuss their importance in the classroom
- When should teachers arrange different seating in the classroom?

Have students respond to each of the questions in writing. Have them form groups of three or four based on the grade levels, and have them share their responses in their respective groups. Then have each group select a member of its group to read the group's response to the whole class. Or you can choose to have individual students share his or her writings in class by reflecting aloud. The purpose of this activity is to stimulate discussion on the topic.

Follow-up Questions/Activity

In light of the reading and discussions, the instructor will ask students to respond in writing to the following:

- Write an outline of a lesson using the insights gained from your reading and the discussions.
- Identify and list a few essential management strategies that will help you deliver better lessons to maximize learning.

Introductory Questions/Activity

- Why is planning important?
- What should planning include?

- When should planning take place?
- Who needs planning most?

Have students respond to each of the questions in writing. Have them form groups of three or four based on the grade levels, and have them share their responses in their respective groups. Then have each group select a member of its group to read the group's response to the whole class. Or you can choose to have individual students share her or his writings in class by reflecting aloud. The purpose of this activity is to stimulate discussion on the topic.

Follow-up Questions/Activity

In light of the reading and discussions, the instructor will ask student teachers to respond in writing the following:

- Write an outline of a lesson using the insights gained from your reading and the discussions.
- Identify and list a few essential management strategies that will help you deliver better lessons to maximize learning.

Introductory Questions/Activity

- What are the essential components in the orchestration of teaching and learning?
- Describe each component and its importance in enhancing learning in the classroom.
- Identify and list components that help you write and deliver better lessons to maximize learning. Have students respond to each of the questions in writing.

Have students form groups of three or four based on the grade levels, and have them share their responses in their respective groups. Then have each group select a member of its group to read the group's response to the whole class. Or you choose to have students share their writings in class by reflecting aloud. The purpose of this activity is to stimulate discussion on the topic.

Follow-up Questions/Activity

In light of the reading and discussions, the instructor will ask student teachers to respond in writing the following:

- Write an outline of a lesson using the insights gained from your reading and the discussions.
- Identify and list a few essential management strategies that will help you deliver better lessons to maximize learning.

Closure

Introductory Questions/Activity

- What is closure?
- Why is closure important?
- What should teachers do in the closure?
- How should teachers end a lesson?

Have students respond to each of the questions in writing. Have them form groups of three or four based on the grade levels, and have them share their responses in their respective groups. Then have each group select a member of their group to read the its response to the whole class. Or you can choose to have individual students share his or her writings in class by reflecting aloud. The purpose of this activity is to stimulate discussion on the topic.

Follow-up Questions/Activity

In light of the reading and discussions, the instructor will ask students to respond in writing the following:

- Write an outline of a lesson using the insights gained from your reading and the discussions.
- Identify and list a few essential management strategies that will help you deliver better lessons to maximize learning.

Effective Social Studies Classroom Culture

One of the challenges faced by faculty in charge of Social Studies Method instruction is how to consistently engage students in activities that equip them with critical-thinking skills. As an approach to help students develop critical-thinking skills and grow as critical-thinking citizens, Critical Thinking-Based Teaching and Learning is based on using topics, cooperative/collaborative inquiry, and reflection as teaching and learning tools. Students' reports and reflection on the projects suggest that (1) more students are actively engaged in their learning, (2) student-student interaction is enhanced, (3) students make connections of the concepts learned with current events and realities in the community, and (4) they stimulate students' ability to reflect and think critically.

To maximize learning, social studies instructors must create learning opportunities that are conducive to free and open inquiry.

Increased Learner Independence

We know that human beings actively construct knowledge and are not merely passive receivers. How, then, do we create an environment of increased learner independence in the classroom?

- Teaching research methodology enables children to look for information to answer questions they have raised; children develop the ability to use firsthand sources gathered in their communities.
- Teachers conduct classroom discussions during which children learn to listen to others as well as express their own views.
- Teachers encourage children to reflect on their own experiences.
- A new role for the teacher is created in which he or she becomes a resource rather than an "answer giver."

Higher-level thinking

To secure intellectual growth, social studies instructors must challenge students by moving beyond lower-level mental exercise questions that require memorization and recitation of specific facts, to higher-order thinking questions that require explanation, evaluation, analysis, and synthesis.

Example: A lower-level mental question may be: What is the capital of United States? Although the answer would be necessary to pass a test, it can go beyond it to ask the student to explain why Washington DC was chosen as the capital of United States.

Provision for Differences in Learners

Teaching situations are characterized by a number of learner differences: intellectual, experiential, social, emotional, preferential, or developmental. To accommodate these differences while presenting a cohesive curriculum is one of the great challenges of teaching any subject. Teachers should view students as people with unique needs, interests, and learning styles—rather than as a potential reservoir for factual knowledge—and provide room for a variety of different learning styles.

Provision of Alternative and Choice

It is ironic that Americans fight and die to defend freedom, yet we deny or allow little freedom to students within education arenas. Allowing some free time to students is a good test to assess how students will use their freedom as responsible citizens (Ellis, 1998).

Promote Success

Not all students in your class will live up to your expectations. For some students, you will need to scale down the scope and difficulty of the task. For others, you may have to intensify the complexity of the task. All students should experience success in order to keep them interested in the lesson or they may become apathetic and may lose interest in learning (Ellis, 1998); they should be rewarded for excellence.

Tips for Effective Management of Classroom Group Discussions

- Group skills and collaborative teamwork are appropriate and required when teaching
- Respect of human differences
- Equity and justice
- Patience for orderly participation
- Social and affective significance
- Openness to others' ideas and perspectives
- Respect for the rights of others
- Sense of responsibility
- Sense of accountability
- Flexibility
- Time management

- Effective time management
- Assign tasks and time
- Introduce flash cards; provide each team with a set.
- Keep a record of the time consistently
- Facilitate learning during group process as needed

Discuss the following issues in your groups, then share with the class the conclusion(s) of your discussion. Support your arguments with factual responses informed by the core democratic values

Topic # 1 Homework
Task: Discuss the following:

- What is homework?
- How much homework is too much?
- What should be the purposes of homework?
- Can different assignments be given to different students in the same class?
- Who is responsible for homework: the students or the parents?
- Do all your students have the same capacity to self-regulate?
- What is the best and most equitable way to deal with overachievers in your class?

Strategy

The jigsaw technique	• Describe advantages of the jigsaw technique. • Task: Describe how you will use it in your Content classroom (the steps). • What challenges do you anticipate?
Self-questioning and think aloud techniques	• Self questioning and think aloud processes are effective strategies to promote problem solving (Baird & White, 1984; Narode, Heiman, Lochead, & Slomianko, 1987). • Task: Think of how you will use them in your content classroom.
Match student study skills to the learning environment	• Occasionally students will have difficulty studying your subject matter topics, yet do very well in other disciplines. • Task: Explain why that may be so. • Suggest ways to help your students.
Cooperative learning	• Not all group work is cooperative learning. • Task: Describe what is cooperative learning and what is not.

Peer-tutoring	• A classroom of students helping other students has been found to be an efficient and effective method of enhancing learning • Task: Before committing to this strategy, what challenged do you need to anticipate?
Gender and ethnic sensitivity	• Classrooms are increasingly characterized by ethnic diversity and this trend will continue to become even stronger • Task: Discuss your biases on gender or ethnicity and how you will overcome it in your classroom
Different motivational strategies for girls and boys	• On average, girls often seem not to be as motivated in science and math as boys • Task: Debate the issue and suggest motivational strategies for boys and girls
Humor in your classroom	• When students are asked to describe exemplary teachers, one of the main characteristics they choose is a sense of humor • Task: Discuss advantages and drawbacks of humor in the classroom
Classroom discipline management	• Tensions can and do exist between personal philosophy and institutionally preferred teacher-student interaction • Examine your teaching philosophy and discuss conflict that you anticipate in your school and the coping strategies you will use to survive
Know your audience	• With the social climate today and students coming to class with a myriad of challenges and concerns, it is more important than ever for teachers to be aware of the problems and challenges of adolescent culture • Task: Discuss strategies you will use to know and understand your students
Teacher talking vs. student talking	• Often teachers fall into the trap of raising their voices to the point of yelling • Task: Discuss strategies you will use to balance your talking with students talking

Classroom time management	• Teachers new to block scheduling need to give special attention to the challenges that longer periods present to your curriculum and pedagogy
	• Task: Discuss the strategies you will use to adjust your instruction to extended class period formats
Post agenda before the start of class	• Using an agenda of the day's lesson makes learning more relevant to students and takes the mystery out of what is going to be covered in class that day
	• Task: Write a sample agenda of your content area in a block scheduling time frame

Questions and Conversation

- What did this class raise for you about interdisciplinary strategies and teaching as a profession?
- How did you feel prior to this class?
- How do you feel going into your classroom?

Assessment of Learning in a Social Studies Classroom

Assessing Knowledge and Understanding

From Benchmarks, Standards, to Grade Level Content Expectations

Standards are stated in ways that make them difficult to address. Some standards are too vast (example) to provide goals, clarity, and guidance to instruction and assessment. Different teachers in good faith emphasize different aspects of the content.

What are the implications for teaching and assessing. They may include:

- Long-term, "authentic projects" (service-learning projects).
- Portfolios (systematic collections of students' work over time).
- Reflective journals/learning logs.
- Informal ongoing observations of students (teacher note-taking, probing questions, exit cards, quick-writes).

Match the Measures with the Goals

- When we want to check for proficiency in skill/process areas such as drawing, writing, or driving (procedural knowledge), then performance assessment items are appropriate evidence.
- For dispositions such as appreciation of the arts, persistence, observations, examples, and portfolios are appropriate to provide appropriate evidence; a quiz on persistence would be an inappropriate measure of such a goal.
- Data on student dispositions or habits of mind and work can yield insights about why a particular student is or is not progressing at a given time; data on student dispositions become important in reporting student progress in a differentiated classroom.

Knowing vs. Understanding

- Knowing is binary—you either know something or you do not.
- Declarative knowledge of facts and concepts falls into this category.
- Understanding is more a matter of degree.
- We speak of someone having a sophisticated insight, a solid grasp, an incomplete or naïve conception, or a misunderstanding.
- When we ask "to what extent does she/he understand?" The answer is revealed along a continuum as shades of gray, rather than black and white. There are implications for how we write our assessment rubrics and how we describe the results.

A challenge for assessing understanding is that it has different connotations.

- They really <u>understand</u> French.
- She <u>understands</u> what I am going through.
- He knows the historical facts but does not <u>understand</u> their significance today.
- I now <u>understand</u> that I never saw the big picture.

The first example suggests ability for someone to use it effectively via listening, speaking, reading, and writing. The second example expresses empathy, the capacity to feel as someone else. The third example implies transfer, the ability to apply what one has learned in a new situation. The fourth example is meta-cognitive: the ability to reflect on one's thinking and learning processes.; clearly it is safe to argue that it is too ambiguous to provide goal clarity and assessment specificity.

Facets of Understanding

When we really understand we can:

- Have perspective (see and hear points of view through different lenses).
- Display empathy (find value in what others find odd, alien).
- Have self-knowledge (show meta-cognitive awareness, perceive prejudices).
- Explain (provide justified accounts of phenomena, facts, and data).
- Interpret (tell meaningful stories, translate).
- Apply/transfer (effectively use and adapt what we know in diverse and real contexts).

It is important to note that explanations need not be exclusively verbal (written or oral). Visual explanations in the form of concept maps, sequence chains, flowcharts, etc., are essential to ensure that students who have strong visual preferences or who struggle with verbal expression have the opportunity to express what they are learning or have learned.

When we call for application, we do not mean mechanical responses to academic prompts. Rather we expect students to use what they know in a new situation, preferably in a real-life context.

Form Follows Function:

- What are we assessing (educational goals)?
- Why are we assessing (rationale, purpose)?
- How are we assessing (matching goals to assessment)?

- For whom are we assessing (accountability)?
- How will the results be used (decisions)?

Purpose

Classroom assessments serve different purposes, one of which is summative. Summative assessments are used to summarize what has been learned. They tend to be evaluative and their results are reported as a score or grade.

Diagnostic and Formative Assessments.

- Are critical for teaching and learning.
- Diagnostic assessment or pre-assessment, precedes instruction and is used to check students' prior knowledge and skill level.
- Identifies misconceptions, interests, or learning-style preferences.
- Provides information to assist teacher planning and guide-differentiated instruction.
- Diagnostic assessments include: (develop some in your groups).

Formative assessments occur concurrently with instruction. Provide information to guide teaching and learning.

Feedback

- Because feedback is directed to the learner, it must be understood.
- Rubrics are feedback tools but sometimes the language in the rubric can be lost on a student.
- What does the instructor mean by "elegant argument" or "sophisticated analysis"?
- Feedback should inform students and guide their improvement.
- Feedback must be clear and comprehensible.
- Develop kid language or developmentally appropriate language rubrics.
- Effective feedback is timely, specific, clear, and allows for adjustment:
- Grades and scores are not feedback.
- B- or 80% on a student's work is no more helpful than comments such as "good job," "way to go," "could do better," etc.
- Good grades may feel good but do not advance learning.
- Because feedback is directed to the learner, it must be understood.
- What does the instructor mean by "elegant argument" or "sophisticated analysis"?
- Feedback should inform students and guide their improvement.
- Feedback must be clear and comprehensible.

If the feedback is not yet specific or understandable enough for the learner, give the learner the opportunity to act on the feedback, to refine, revise, etc.

   a. **Assessment rubric** (field related). University coordinators will use the assessment rubric as a basis for observing and assessing individual student-teacher's management effectiveness. Student-teachers can also use the rubric as a reference to assess their personal management effectiveness on daily basis.

b. **Self-assessment form** (field related). University coordinators will use the self-assessment form to record in writing the feedback on the management performance of individual student-teachers.

c. **Reflective assignments**. Students will use this form to assess their own classroom management performance based on the listed categories.

The self-assessment activity and the reflective assignments will enable student-teachers to assess their professional growth in classroom management and provide them with items they need to develop in their professional portfolios.

The Purpose of Feedback

Giving verbal or written feedback to students is essential in helping them realize the quality of the work they submitted. It helps them realize what they have accomplished and what they need to work on. The grade is a form of feedback, but alone it is not enough to judge the progress of students. It only segregates students in arbitrary categories. Evaluating students' work by allocating points, percentages, or letter grades without a qualitative written feedback to justify the grade is doing a disservice to students. Likewise, when giving feedback it is important to consider questions that can inform helpful feedback.

Can the students tell specifically from the given feedback where they have done well and what they could do next time to improve?

If not, the feedback is not yet specific or understandable enough for the learner; give the learner the opportunity to act on the feedback, to refine and revise his or her work in order to improve his or her grade.

Assessing the Standards Effectively

The primary goal of evaluation is to acknowledge the accomplishments of students and the teaching objectives of the instructor. For students to achieve learning expectations successfully, they must have ready access to relevant grade-level learning materials and to a knowledgeable and open-minded instructor. The instructor should assume the role of facilitator by providing rationale and purpose for learning the material at hand.

Access	Sample instructional guidelines
Access to content	• Students need to have access to the knowledge and skills described in the standards.

Access to teachers	• Students need access to teachers who are knowledgeable about the disciplines they teach, about the developmental characteristics of the students they teach, and about best practices in learning and teaching. For example, accessibility and knowledge is when a teacher plans developmentally appropriate curriculum and instruction, and presents accurate knowledge through multiple perspectives and connected disciplines.
	• Students also need access to teachers who share their knowledge, work with colleagues, and who are continually learning. For example, when a teacher participates in a variety of professional development experiences to increase his or her knowledge.
	• Teachers work with others (parents, students, content-area experts, colleagues) to plan and assess the curriculum.
Access to resources	• Students need equitable and prompt access to accurate and relevant materials and current resources at school and in the community. For example, frequent opportunities to engage the community as a resource and a learning laboratory (such as artists, businesses, health care providers, town meetings, etc.)
Access to time	• Students need instruction that uses time effectively, and flexibly to achieve learning goals. For example, evidence of that is when: - Schedules are built around learning and instructional needs (flexible blocks). - Downtime is used in creative and purposeful ways. - Time is built in for collaboration (e.g. student with teacher, teacher with teacher, teacher with parent). - Maximum time is devoted to student time-on-task and in-depth learning.
Access to a safe and healthy environment	• Students need to learn in an environment that is physically and emotionally safe and educationally supportive. For example, equipment, work, and learning spaces are maintained and organized so that tasks and projects are carried out safely. • Adults are healthy and model healthy behaviors • Each student has access to a caring adult. • Policies and rules are fair, known to all, and consistently applied.

Instruction	• Students need learning experiences that engage them in active learning, build on prior knowledge and experiences, and develop conceptual and procedural understanding. For example: - Begin learning experiences by setting a context or previewing possible applications. - Use strategies that help students link new learning to previous knowledge and experiences (such as discussion of previous experiences, free writes, pre-tests, think-pair-share, etc.). - Scaffold learning (remove cues over time as students learn to converse in a second language). - Prompt students to support their statements with evidence (during comparison, classification, and construction to support position). - Use strategies that help students organize and interpret new learning (have students create graphs and charts, graphic organizers, etc.). - Use questions that extend and refine learning (open-ended questions, error-analysis questions). - Provide opportunities for students to bring up and explore their own misconceptions and to replace these with accurate conceptions of knowledge.
Assuming multiple teaching roles	• A teacher can assume the following roles: a direct instructor, facilitator, model, coach, reflective practitioner guide, observer, etc. For example, assume a role determined by the purpose of the learning and the needs of the students.
Assuming multiple learning roles (students)	• Students need opportunities to learn through a variety of roles such as planner, questioner, artist, scientist, historian, etc.). For example, have students learn in small and large groups. • Teach other students, formally and informally. • Pursue personal learning interests and projects. • Design learning activities with peers. • Participate in field trips.

Application and reflection	• Projects and assignments require students to integrate and apply their learning in meaningful contexts and to reflect on what they have learned, e.g., when students participate in extended inquiries through which they address essential questions.
	• Transfer learning from one format or context to another.
	• Design products.
	• Plan activities and carry out projects that meet real needs.
	• Use in-depth applications through critique and interpretations of others' ideas.
	• Perform reflection through different modes such as writing, talking, singing, dancing, painting, etc.
Assessment and reporting	• Assessment strategies used to gain information and provide feedback about student learning include: performance assessment, self-assessment, paper-and-pencil test, checklist, etc.
Assessment criteria	• Expectations and performance criteria should be clear and public. For example, clearly define student products or performances and judge with observable criteria based on standards.
	• Publicly display student work samples on walls, bookmarks, newsletters.
Assessment should inform instruction and guide student learning	• Assessment results are used to influence instructional decisions and to plan students' next learning steps.
	• Classroom-based assessments are embedded into instruction. For example, assessment of prior knowledge about a topic, entries in learning logs.
Student involvement in assessment	• Students use clear criteria to evaluate their own work. For example, use rubrics to assess cooperative group activities.

Communicate assessment information effectively	• To effectively communicate critical information:
	  - Summarize assessments in relation to standards.
	  - Share results with, and report to students, parents, and other professionals.
	  - Compare student achievement with standards, showing student's growth over time and public accountability.

	• Assessment must be fair, valid, and consistent (reliable).
	• Report card reflects student progress toward the standard over time, as well as student achievement of the standards.
	• Students are involved in parent conferences.
Connections	• Strategies

Interdisciplinary connections	• Engage students in:
	- Direct experience with real-world questions, problems, issues that cross discipline limits. For example, questioning, estimating, technical writing used in social and physical sciences.
	- Vocabulary study connected with the history of the English language.
	- Investigation of problems that lend themselves to the scope of interdisciplinary work (study of rural economic development from social, economic, and environmental perspectives).
Relevance	• Learning experiences have personal, community, or global relevance.
	• Use thematic studies that allow students to draw connections between their lives and the world beyond the classroom. For example, the study of immigration patterns in a local town, using the outdoor classroom to learn the natural heritage of a local community.
	• Service-learning experiences that are linked to classroom learning (writing a resource book for younger students).
Collaborating with family and community	• Collaboration includes:
	- Ongoing, two-way communication with parents.
	- A variety of learning environments in the community are used. (Libraries, lumberyards, shops, historical societies, forests, watersheds, etc.)
	- Connections across generations (mentoring, foster-grandparents).
	- Flexible scheduling for parent-teacher conferences.
	- Home visits to meet the needs of the families.
	- Evidence of recognition and support of diverse languages and cultures (interpreters at open houses and parent-teacher conferences).
Best practices in the fields of knowledge	• Strategies
Language, literature	• Emphasis on multiple reading strategies and comprehension.
	• Writing (letters, free writes, learning logs.)
	• Allowing self-selected topics, materials, grouping patterns, books.
	• Respecting and providing support for languages and dialects used in students' homes.

History and social sciences	• Best practices specific to history and the social science include:
	  • Opportunities to participate in democratic processes in the school and the community.
	  • Opportunities to collaborate with people of various cultures and social classes.
	  • Access to national and international organizations.

Science, mathematics, and technology	• Best practices specific to science, mathematics, and technology include:
	  - Use of manipulatives and scientific tools (calculators, microscopes, graphing calculators, computer, tan grams).
	  - Engaging students in active, in-depth learning (inquiries, problem solving).
	  - Frequent interactions with the natural world.
	  - Inquiry, investigation, experimentation as a regular part of the science program.
	  - Frequent oral and written interactions between teacher and students and among students to develop deep thinking in math and science (discussions, presentations, learning logs, open-ended follow-up questions).
	  - Teacher displays scientist's habits of mind, such as skepticism, rigor in data collection, and peer review.
	  - Basic skills such as measuring, recording, and computing integrated with analysis, synthesis, and evaluation.
	  - Opportunities for students to present the results of their investigations to peers for review and critique.

Objective Testing Questions

Direction: In your group, identify at least four objective testing questions and describe their advantages and drawbacks

Advantages	*Drawbacks*
• Can evaluate skills quickly and efficiently	• Requires mostly recall of facts
• Can prevent students from writing around the answer	• Does not allow students to demonstrate writing skills.
• Can prevent students' grades from being influenced by writing skills, spelling, grammar, and neatness	• Penalizes poor readers

- Can be easily analyzed

- Prevents biased grading by teacher

- Can be used for diagnostic or pre-test purposes

- Can be given to a large groups

- Other

- Ambiguous and confusing

- Always has a specific predetermined answer

- Can be time consuming to construct

- Promotes guessing

- Is used year after year despite differing needs of students

- Other

Guidelines for Teacher-developed Tests

Make sure the test is correlated to the course objectives or learning outcomes. Give clear directions for each section of the test. Arrange the questions from simple to complex, concrete to abstract. Give point values for each section (e.g., true/false, 2 points each). Vary the question types (true/false, fill-in-the-blanks, multiple choice, essay, matching, etc.). Group question types together. Leave space between questions to facilitate easy reading and writing. Include a variety of visual, oral, and kinesthetic tasks. Make provisions for students with special needs. Give students some choice (e.g., graphic organizer or essay). Provide the grading scale and give sufficient time for all students to complete the task at hand.

Graphic Organizer

Directions: Complete the mind map on _____ by filling in the main components in the big circles and the subpoints in the smaller circles. (1 point per circle).

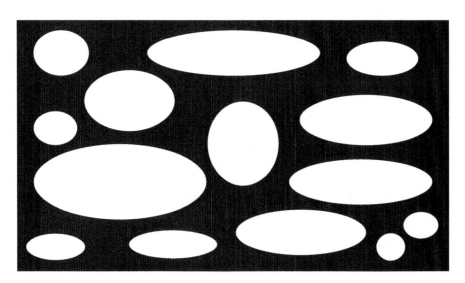

Essay Question

Point value: 20

Directions: Select one of the following topics for your essay question. Your essay will be evaluated on the following criteria:

    a.   accuracy of information
    b.   organization of information
    c.   use of support statements
    d.   clarity and effectiveness

Select one topic.

1.   Predict what will happen if the ozone layer continues to deplete at its current rate.
2.   Evaluate the effectiveness of our government's research and regulations regarding acid rain.
3.   Speculate what will happen if a cure for AIDS is not found within five years.
4.   Compare and contrast the bubonic plague to AIDS. You may draw a Venn diagram to help you organize your thoughts before you write.

Critique Criteria of the Group Test Design

Directions: Read the checklist and check those that apply.

Test _____

Grade level: _____ Topic _____

1.   The question types are varied._____
2.   A point value is given for each section._____
3.   Test items are arranged from simple to complex. _____
4.   Tasks for visual, auditory, and kinesthetic learners are included._____
5.   Students are given a choice of questions._____
6.   Provision is made for students with special needs._____
7.   Time is adequately allocated for completion of the tasks by all students._____
8.   The grading scale is listed._____

Comments:

Portfolios

Premise: A portfolio is more than a folder full of stuff. It is a systematic and organized collection of evidence used by the teacher and the students to monitor growth of the student's knowledge, skills, and attitudes in a specific subject area.

Example # 1 Language Arts Portfolio
Integrated Unit

Table of Contents

1. Letter to parents
2. Book review
3. Semantic/mind map of spiders
4. Tape of me reading a story
5. Science report
6. Spider rap song
7. Pictures of group project on spiders
8. Reflections on my portfolio

Subject: Science project   Final grade: _____

Grade	Descriptors
5	The subject is addressed clearly
	Speech is loud enough and easy to understand
	Good eye contact
	Visual aid is used effectively
	Well organized
4	Subject is addressed adequately
	Speech has appropriate volume
	Eye contact is intermittent
	Visual aid helps presentation
	Good organization
3	Subject is addressed adequately
	Speech volume is erratic
	Student reads notes
	Erratic eye contact
	Visual aid does not enhance speech
	Speech gets off track at times

2   Speech needs more explanation

Speech is difficult to understand at times

Lack of adequate eye contact

Poor visual aid

Lack of organization

1   Speech does not address topic

Speech cannot be heard

Very little eye contact

No visual aid

No organization

Scale: 5= A; 4= B; 3= C; 2= D.

General comments: You did a good job demonstrating your project and delivering the speech. Your organization, however, was a little sloppy and you read your notes too much.

Qualitative Scales

Use adjectives rather than numbers to characterize student's performance. There are two types of qualitative scales: descriptive and evaluative.

Descriptive Scale

Label student performance by using neutral terms to characterize the performance. Example:

- No evidence (NE); Minimal evidence (ME); Partial evidence (PE); Complete evidence (CE).
- Task not attempted; Partial completion; Completed; Goes beyond.
- Off task; Attempts to address task; Minimal attention to task; Addresses task but no elaboration; Fully elaborated and attentive to task.

Evaluative Scale

Incorporate judgments of worth based on standards of excellence.

The most commonly used evaluative scales are grades. Other evaluative scales use descriptors of excellence or judgment of competence. Example:

Grade	Descriptors
A	Student addressed topic logically and used effective delivery style to present case.
B	Student addressed topic in organized way and used effective speaking techniques.
C	Student addressed topic but did not use effective speaking techniques (eye contact, gestures).
D	Student did not address the topic.
F	Student did not give speech.

What will we accept as evidence of student understanding and proficiency?

Step one: Identify desired outcome (s): What should/will students know, understand, and be able to do and develop as a result of your instruction?

Step two: Determine acceptable evidence: How will you or an observer in your classroom know whether or not students have learned?

Step three: Plan learning experiences and instruction. What activities, sequence, and resources are best suited to accomplish our goals?

- The main goal is to engage children with a learning purpose while keeping the end in mind.
- The activities should yield evidence of learning.
- Elementary is often activity-oriented.
- Secondary is coverage. A chronological march through the textbook.
- Planning backward focuses on teaching and learning of important content.
- Checking regularly for understanding on the part of all students.
- Make needed adjustments based on the results.

What really matters in planning for instruction:

- It is vital to be clear about what is essential in content.
- What have experts identified as core of a discipline?
- Clarity about what really matters help us to teach for understanding.
- To teach for understanding is to teach content and people.

Differentiated Instruction

- All students should have access to a curriculum rich with the ideas and skills valued by experts in their fields.
- There are many ways to teach students; there are many ways to support students' learning.
- Teach to students' variances.
- Few teachers translate these ideals into classroom.
- Efforts and commitment to move from current practice to desired practice.
- Establish clarity about curricular essentials.
- Accept responsibility for students' success.
- Develop communities of respect.
- Develop awareness of what works for individual students.
- Develop classroom-management routines that contribute to effective learning. Develop flexible classroom teaching routines.
- Expand a repertoire of instructional strategies.
- Reflect on individual progress by assessing mastery of curricular goals.
- There is no such thing as a perfect lesson, a perfect day, or a perfect teacher.
- The goal is not perfection but persistence in the pursuit of understanding important things; that is the essence of expert teaching.
- Evidence of learning in diverse classrooms.
- Anyone concerned about teaching and learning should also be interested in assessment.
- Did the student learn? To what extent?
- How can we maintain standards without standardization?
- Purpose of assessment.

Assessment

- Process by which we make inferences about what students know, understand, and can do based on information obtained through assessment.
- A single test at the end of instruction is less likely to provide a complete picture of a student's learning. Reliable assessment demands multiple sources of evidence.
- Multiple assessments are essential because no one test can do it all; no test, no matter how good it is, should be the sole criterion for any decision.

Teaching Critical Thinking

- Politically driven motives rely on "quick-fix" standardized tests as a basis for judging students, schools, and districts. There is nothing inherently wrong with standardized tests.
- Standardized tests provide useful comparable data about students' achievement levels. The problem is when the results of a single test are used to make high-stakes decisions. The pressures to improve test scores can lead to a narrowing of the curriculum toward the tested topics and an overemphasis on test prep at the expense of meaningful learning.
- Oral communication, decision-making, research, expression in the arts are not tested.
- The standardized nature "one-size-fits-all" of most large-scale testing flies in the face of what we know—children learn differently at different paces.

Implications for Teaching and Assessing

- In the context of the classroom we can use a variety of assessments to document evidence of learning (McTighe and Wiggins, 2004).
- Selected-response format (multiple choice, true/false) quizzes and tests.
- Written or oral responses to prompts (short-answer formats). Performance assessment tasks:
  - Extended written products (essays, lab reports).
  - Visual products (PowerPoint presentations, Prezies, murals).
  - Oral performances (oral reports, foreign language dialogues).
  - Demonstrations (skill performances in PE).
- Long-term, "authentic projects" (service-learning projects).
- Portfolios (systematic collections of students' work over time).
- Reflective journals/learning logs.
- Informal ongoing observations of students (teacher note-taking, probing questions, exit cards, quick-writes).
- Formal observations of students using observable indicators or criterion list.
- Student self-assessment.
- Peer reviews and peer response groups.
- Caution and Recommendations: It is not suggested that everything we teach requires multiple assessments. But more than a single source of evidence is needed in academically diverse classrooms where different students have a chance to demonstrate their knowledge, understanding, and skills in different formats.
- In standards-based education, the rubber meets the road with assessment.
- Get colleagues on board to work in teams.
- Find agreement on both the goals and on the needed assessment evidence of meeting these goals.
- Multiple assessments are important as a matter of sensitivity for learner variance.
- Assessment Principle Two: Match the measures with the goals
- Educational goals:
  - Declarative knowledge: what students should know and understand.
  - Procedural knowledge: what students should be able to do.
  - Dispositions: what attitudes or habits of mind (Marzano, 1992) students should display.

If we want to see whether or not students know multiplication tables or chemical symbols (declarative knowledge), then objective test items such as multiple-choice, matching, true/false, or fill-in-the-blanks will provide appropriate evidence. When we want to check for proficiency in skill/process areas such as drawing, writing, or driving (procedural knowledge), then performance assessment items are appropriate evidence. For dispositions, such as appreciation of the arts, persistence, observations, examples, and portfolios are appropriate to provide appropriate evidence.

A quiz on persistence would be an appropriate measure of such a goal in a different kind of classroom or differentiated classroom; it is essential to attend to student proficiency with all three kinds of knowledge.

- Need to use assessment data on individual students to map our instructional plan.

- Data on student dispositions or habits of mind and work can yield insights about why a particular student is or is not progressing at a given time.
- Data on student dispositions become important in reporting student progress in a differentiated classroom

Documenting Learning in Social Studies

Prior to 1930, social studies was concerned with a body of facts to be memorized. Little or no reflection was done about those facts. Teachers used lecture and discussion as the main methodology for teaching social studies. The reflection is at the heart of Social Studies Method instruction because it provides evidence of learning as experienced by individual students in his or her own words.

Social Studies Goals and Expectations of Social Studies Education.

Knowledge and Information Goals

Student will learn about:

1. The world, its geography, people, cultures.
2. The history, settlement, growth, and development of the United States.
3. The neighborhood, community, home state; how people live and work there; how they meet their basic needs of life; how they interact and depend on each other.
4. The legal and political system of the local community, the state, and the nation.
5. The world of work and orientation to various careers.
6. Basic human institutions, such as the family.
7. How people use and misuse natural resources.
8. The problems and challenges that confront people today in the realm of social living and human relations in the local, state, national, and international arenas.
9. The basic social functions that characterize all societies such as producing, transporting, distributing, and consuming goods and services; providing for education, recreation, and government; protecting and conserving human and natural resources; expressing esthetic and religious drives; communicating with others.

Attitude and Value Goals

Students will:

1. Know about the common values of this society as defined in the Constitution, the law of the land, the courts, and the religions of this country.
2. Be able to make decisions that involve choices between competing values.
3. Know the basic human rights guaranteed to all citizens.
4. Develop a reasoned loyalty to this country.
5. Develop a sense of respect for the ideals, heritages, and institutions of this nation.
6. Develop a feeling of kinship toward human beings everywhere.

Skills Goals
a. Social skills
Will be able to:

1. Live and work together; take turns; respect the rights of others; be socially sensitive.
2. Learn self-control and self-direction.
3. Share ideas and experiences with others

b. Study skills and work habits
Will be able to:

1. Use maps, globes, charts, graphs, graphic and pictorial materials.
2. Locate and gather information from a variety of sources.
3. Write and read reports, make public speeches, listen when others are reporting.
4. Read social studies materials for diverse purposes.
5. Organize information into usable structures such as outlines, charts, time lines; classify, sequence, take notes, keep records, write summaries.
6. Conduct inquiry on a problem of interest.

c. Group work skills
Students will be able to:

1. Work cooperatively in groups and on committees, and assume various roles in small groups such as chairperson, secretary, or committee member.
2. Participate in group discussion; lead a discussion.
3. Participate in group decision making.

d. Intellectual skills
Students will be able to:

1. Define and identify problems; relate prior experience to present inquiry.
2. Form and test hypotheses; draw conclusions based on information.
3. Analyze and synthesize data.
4. Think critically; distinguish between fact and opinion. Learn to separate relevant from irrelevant information; recognize bias in persuasive materials such as advertising, political statements, and propaganda.
5. Sense cause-and-effect relationships.
6. Compare differing points of view.

Note: Creative thinking and problem solving are associated with the American ethos. Americans are stereotyped as creative and problem solvers (Jarolimek, 1990).

The ultimate goal of education is to prepare individuals to make decisions, to make judgments, and to lead lives that are qualitatively superior to those who are uneducated. Educated people should be able to distinguish between what is true and what is not, what is better than something else, what enhances the human condition and what does not, and what is morally uplifting and what is not. These kinds of discriminations in quality are what schools and education are supposed to equip students to make. If there were no qualitative differences between the lives of people who went to school and those who did not, society would do away with schools.

Much of social studies teaching is directed toward the achievement of more than one objective at the same time.

Characteristics of Effective Social Studies

- The subject matter is drawn from history, geography, and a broad range of social sciences.
- The experiences of children are essential parts of the learning activities.
- A global perspective is apparent throughout discussions, with attention to non-western cultures as well as those of the west.
- Lessons involving challenging activities calling for active learner participation are used.
- Application of what is learned in the classroom is transferred to out-of-school settings through social action participation.
- There is use of multiple instructional resources.
- Deep and critical thinking is emphasized as the major concern of social studies instruction; students are provided many opportunities for creative and critical thinking and for decision making.
- Diversity is treated as a social reality at home and abroad, and the contributions of different cultures to humankind are celebrated.
- A genuine effort is made in developing knowledge, skills, and beliefs and values.
- Truthful pictures of social reality are shown to dispel biases and stereotypes.
- Core democratic values are the basis for classroom discussions.
- Many options are available to the teacher in terms of various programs, materials, and teaching strategies.
- The instructional planning format is an interdisciplinary study around a theme, a current event, a topic of interest to students.

Social studies experiences can help children understand and appreciate the various lifestyles of the human race through direct contact with artifacts and people from cultures other than their own. Resources needed to provide such experiences are now available in most American communities. Today, children learn about social studies from their lives outside the classroom, through travel, television, the Internet, and contact with adults. Hardly anything encountered in social studies will be totally new to all children. As a result social studies should be taught from what children already know.

When children are studying the local landscape, they are dealing in a simple way with geography. When they learn about the need for rules and laws, they are studying political science. When they study about life in early times, they are learning history. It is not the purpose of social studies to teach social sciences apart from their relevance to social reality. Social studies should be taught in ways that help children build an understanding of the social and physical world in which they live.

Social studies has been part of the elementary curriculum for decades, yet it is not an easy subject to define (Maxim, 2003). To begin with, it is essential to consider the difference between the terms "social science" and "social studies." The word "science" is derived from the Latin word *scientia*, which means knowledge. Therefore social science may be defined as any of the fields that seek to understand and explain the social realm of human existence (Maxim, 2003). These include geography, history, political science, sociology, anthropology, and economics. To understand and explain human existence, social scientists conduct research using different methodologies, including field investigations; living and working among people being researched; examining historical documents, artifacts, and records; creating and interpreting maps; administering tests and questionnaires; and conducting interviews and surveys.

If our goals are to prepare young people to acquire skills and operate like social scientists such as anthropologists, historians, and what have you, we must first acquire skills and knowledge about the roles of historians and geographers in order to make adequate methodological and instructional decisions in teaching social studies.

Higher-level Thinking

To secure intellectual growth, teachers must challenge students by moving beyond lower-level mental exercise questions that require memorization and recitation of specific facts to higher-order thinking questions that require explanation, evaluation, and analysis.

Example: A lower-level mental question may be: What is the capital of the United States? Although the answer would be necessary to pass a test, it can go beyond to ask the student to explain why Washington DC was chosen as the capital of United States.

Provision for Differences in Learners

Teaching situations are characterized by a number of learner differences: intellectual, experiential, social, emotional, preferential, and developmental. To accommodate these differences while presenting a cohesive curriculum is one of the great challenges of teaching any subject. Teachers should view students as people with unique needs, interests, and learning styles—rather than as a potential reservoir for factual knowledge—and provide room for a variety of different learning styles.

Give students freedom:

- It is ironic that Americans fight and die to defend freedom, yet we deny or allow little freedom to students within education arenas. Allowing some free time to students is a good test to assess how students will use their freedom as responsible citizens (Ellis, 1998).

Promote success:

- Not all students in your class will live up to your expectations. For some students, you will need to scale down the scope and difficulty of the task. For others, you may have to intensify the complexity of the task. All students should experience success in order to keep them interested in the lesson or they may become apathetic and may lose interest in learning (Ellis, 1998).

Reward excellence:

- Make the work of your students visible. Display their work and promote public recognition and appreciation for excellence.

Historically, several influences seem to play key roles in the shaping of the social studies curriculum. While the nineteenth and twentieth centuries have been dominated by traditional social studies curricula focused on the mastery of low-level mental exercise questions that yield recitations of facts such as names of the rivers, capital cities, and important dates, the twenty-first century is marked with the emergence of new problems, values, and concerns that present new challenges to the social studies curriculum and teaching methodology.

The traditional curriculum focused on Eurocentric cultural experiences, values, and the preservation of these values through transmission methodology.

A twenty-first century social studies curriculum should be consistent with the current issues and values, and the methodology should challenge students with higher-order thinking questions and promote alternative views of the world from the lenses of the non-western citizens.

Social studies instruction is a broad field that is becoming more and more integrated with other content areas. Therefore the scope needs to focus on basic, specific, and critical topics.

Assumptions:

- Teacher candidates come into the professional sequence of their teacher preparation programs with a general knowledge or background in academic disciplines such as history, sociology, geography, etc., which serves as a foundation for elementary social studies.
- Teachers are scheduled for only one-semester, one- to three-credit courses in teaching social studies, or a core methods course in which social studies instruction is integrated.
- Teachers have other courses in the program that expose them to learning theory, lesson planning, and instructional technology.

Learning activities in social studies:

- Clipping out items from a newspaper for Friday current events.
- Doing a research report on "X" using an encyclopedia.
- Finding out the latitude and longitude of cities on a list.
- Learning about the pilgrims at Thanksgiving.
- Writing a contest essay on American government.
- Answering questions at the end of a textbook chapter.
- Reenacting pioneer life.

Learners as individuals will develop over time into active citizens. Social studies is an area of the curriculum deriving its goals from the nature of citizenship in a democratic society with links to other societies. Drawing its content from the social sickness and other disciplines, social studies also incorporates the personal and social experiences of students and their cultural heritage. It links factors outside the individual with factors inside the individual, particularly the development and use of reflective thinking, problem solving, and rational decision-making skills for the purpose of creating involvement in social action (pp. 7–8). Social action is a continuum of possible activities ranging from single efforts requiring small commitments of time and talent to long-term projects requiring a regular commitment of time and multiple intellectual and social skills. These possible activities can involve regularly picking up litter, reading stories to children in younger grades during rainy lunch times, making Valentine's Day cards for nursing home residents, washing dishes at a soup kitchen for homeless people, or working to have stop sign installed at a busy intersection where school children cross. Prior to engaging in those activities, students must be made aware of the projects and understand the rationale for doing them

Over the years the content of the elementary curriculum has expanded to meet and keep pace with the social ethos, demographic shifts, and new research findings about teaching and learning. Consequently, a greater sociocultural understanding, an attitude of care and concern, a willingness to participate in social criticism and critical self-reflection, and a commitment to engage in personal actions serve an increasing number of others (Houser, 1999).

The content of best practice with Cubberly's 1920 representation of the elementary curriculum shows that educational goals have evolved to outlive the best practice. For example, social studies today seems to be tied to social disciplines. In other words, the core subjects of history, geography, and civics have expanded to include all the social sciences disciplines that were singled out and taught in isolation. Today teachers are encouraged or urged to connect and integrate social sickness across the content areas. Likewise teachers are expected to teach content areas in depth and in scope by integrating other content areas.

When goals are couched as such with expectations to teach for in-depth understanding and breadth, it becomes legitimate for social studies teachers to wonder how these goals can realistically be met in one subject area when operationally social studies is only one aspect of the entire school day. As one teacher put it "we have curricular obesity and everyone wants to add more" (McEachron, 2001, p. 9).

In 1966, the Social Sciences Education Consortium developed and joined the fundamental ideas or structures of economics, political sciences, sociology, anthropology, and geography. The structures were expected to be part of the teacher education programs as they have become the core content in social studies for several decades. The concepts seem to overlap from one subject to another.

Hence, combining the same concepts that many subject matters address would lead to a multi-disciplinary approach. For example, a thematic unit plan on families would incorporate concepts from history, economics, political sciences, sociology, anthropology, geography, and psychology.

Cooperative learning (Farris Cooper):

- Noncompetitive
- Stimulates student interactions

- Contributions highly expected from individual members
- Critical social skill
- Hours of interactive learning
- Empowers students
- Places responsibility for learning on students

Cooperative or collaborative learning (Chapin, J.R. and Messick, G.R.):

- Students work together in small groups on a common topic or problem
- Exchange and evaluate data, ideas
- Learn or review new material
- Students learn from their peers, improve intergroup relations.
- Viable instructional method to use to deliver content and teach skills
- Individual accountability
- Allows no free ride

Inquiry process/problem solving = student-centered instruction vs. teacher-centered instruction (lecture to present information; recitation to test, orally retained information) Welton, D.A. (2002).

The back-to-basics era (1970s and 1980s) and NCLB mandates have negatively influenced social studies because it was disappearing from early elementary.

The major mission of social studies education is to help children learn about the social world in which they live, and develop skills, attitudes, and knowledge to act on solving problems to improve their social world. Social studies focuses on citizenship education, which means learning to participate in group life (Jarolimek, 1990). Social studies aims at attaining two sometimes contradictory ends. On the one hand, socialization, through which citizens internalize values and attitudes, causes them to behave willingly in accordance with prevailing expectations and norms. This is a basic requirement for orderly social life. On the other hand, citizens also have the obligation to be critical of the system itself in order that basic rights and freedom can be sustained and extended to all citizens through social criticism.

Teaching socialization and social criticism can be a challenge. On the one hand we want citizens to obey the law, but we do not want them to be intimidated by the law or those who enforce the law. Citizens in a democratic society are expected to support individuals whom they have elected into office. At the same time citizens have a responsibility to hold accountable their elected officials and not follow them blindly when their leadership turns into demagoguery. Teachers must find a balance between the two expectations when teaching citizenship at elementary and middle levels. If our goals are to prepare young people to acquire skills and operate like social scientists such as anthropologists, historians, and what have you, we must first acquire skills and knowledge about the roles of historians and geographers in order to make adequate methodological and instructional decisions in teaching social studies.

ACTIVITIES

The Pursuit of Happiness

A person has the right to find happiness in his or her own way as long as he or she does not step on the rights of others.

Points Stimulating Discussion

1. After reading each of the core democratic values, think of instances in everyday life when this value is undermined.
2. Think of instances historically when people did not live up to this value.
3. Describe the daily life and the historical contexts in which it occurred.
4. After reading each of the core democratic values, think of instances in everyday life when the value is celebrated.
5. Think of instances historically when people lived up to this value.
6. Describe the daily life and the historical contexts in which it occurred.

ACTIVITES

Patriotism

Citizens should show respect and loyalty to our country and the core democratic values.

ACTIVITES

Questions to Stimulate Discussion

1. After reading each of the core democratic values, think of instances in everyday life when this value is undermined.
2. Think of instances historically when people did not live up to this value.
3. Describe the daily life and the historical contexts in which it occurred.
4. After reading each of the core democratic values, think of instances in everyday life when the value is celebrated.
5. Think of instances historically when people lived up to this value.
6. Describe the daily life and the historical contexts in which it occurred.

Justice

All people should be treated fairly when correcting wrongs or injuries and when making decisions. No group should be favored.

Questions to Stimulate Discussion

1. After reading each of the core democratic values, think of instances in everyday life when this value is undermined.
2. Think of instances historically when people did not live up to this value.
3. Describe the daily life and the historical contexts in which it occurred.
4. After reading each of the core democratic values, think of instances in everyday life when the value is celebrated.
5. Think of instances historically when people lived up to this value.
6. Describe the daily life and the historical contexts in which it occurred.

ACTIVITES

Life

An individual has the right to life, except in extreme cases, such as the use of deadly force to protect one's own or others' lives.

Questions to Stimulate Discussion

1. After reading each of the core democratic values, think of instances in everyday life when this value is undermined.
2. Think of instances historically when people did not live up to this value.
3. Describe the daily life and the historical contexts in which it occurred.
4. After reading each of the core democratic values, think of instances in everyday life when the value is celebrated.
5. Think of instances historically when people lived up to this value.
6. Describe the daily life and the historical contexts in which it occurred.

ACTIVITES

Popular Sovereignty

The power of the government comes from the people.

Questions to Stimulate Discussion

1. After reading each of the core democratic values, think of instances in everyday life when this value is undermined.
2. Think of instances historically when people did not live up to this value.
3. Describe the daily life and the historical contexts in which it occurred.
4. After reading each of the core democratic values, think of instances in everyday life when the value is celebrated.
5. Think of instances historically when people lived up to this value.
6. Describe the daily life and the historical contexts in which it occurred.

ACTIVITES

Diversity

Variety in culture and ethnic background, race, lifestyle, and belief is not only permissible but desirable and beneficial in a pluralist society.

Questions to Stimulate Discussion

1. After reading each of the core democratic values, think of instances in everyday life when this value is undermined.
2. Think of instances historically when people did not live up to this value.
3. Describe the daily life and the historical contexts in which it occurred.
4. After reading each of the core democratic values, think of instances in everyday life when the value is celebrated.
5. Think of instances historically when people lived up to this value.
6. Describe the daily life and the historical contexts in which it occurred.

ACTIVITES

The Common Good

Citizens should work together for the good of all. The government should make laws that are good for everyone.

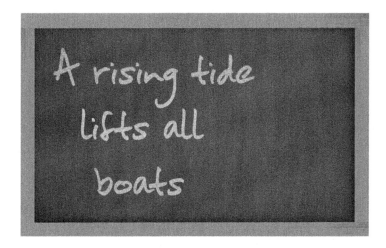

Questions to Stimulate Discussion

1. After reading each of the core democratic values, think of instances in everyday life when this value is undermined.
2. Think of instances historically when people did not live up to this value.
3. Describe the daily life and the historical contexts in which it occurred.
4. After reading each of the core democratic values, think of instances in everyday life when the value is celebrated.
5. Think of instances historically when people lived up to this value.
6. Describe the daily life and the historical contexts in which it occurred.

ACTIVITES

Liberty

A person has the freedom to act, to think, and to believe as he or she wants without the government interfering. This includes the right for the people to meet in groups and express ideas in public.

Questions to Stimulate Discussion

1. After reading each of the core democratic values, think of instances in everyday life when this value is undermined.
2. Think of instances historically when people did not live up to this value.
3. Describe the daily life and the historical contexts in which it occurred.
4. After reading each of the core democratic values, think of instances in everyday life when the value is celebrated.
5. Think of instances historically when people lived up to this value.
6. Describe the daily life and the historical contexts in which it occurred.

ACTIVITES

Truth

The government and citizens should not lie. Citizens can legitimately demand that telling the truth, refraining from lying, and full disclosure by government be the rule.

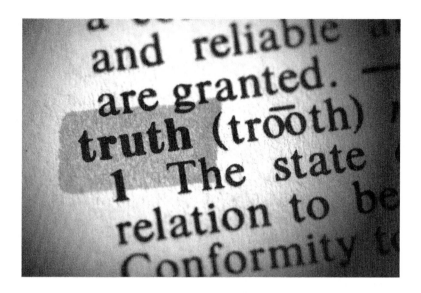

Questions to Stimulate Discussion

1. After reading each of the core democratic values, think of instances in everyday life when this value is undermined.
2. Think of instances historically when people did not live up to this value.
3. Describe the daily life and the historical contexts in which it occurred.

Equality

Everybody should get the same treatment regardless of where they are from, their race, their religion, or how much money they have.

Questions to Stimulate Discussion

1. After reading each of the core democratic values, think of instances in everyday life when this value is undermined.
2. Think of instances historically when people did not live up to this value.
3. Describe the daily life and the historical contexts in which it occurred.

ACTIVITES

LESSON PLANS

Lesson Plan Template

(Disclaimer): There is no single lesson plan format to follow; this is just one format that you will use in this class. You can use other formats that suit your teaching style. Each format has its own vocabulary. Whatever format you choose MUST contain at least the following steps.

Sample #1

NAME_____ School_____

Curriculum Area_____ Grade level_____ Date _____

Lesson Title:

Teaching Goal(s): BIG IDEA or Purpose

GLCE(s):

Learning Objective(s): The learning objectives must focus on three different domains:

1. Cognitive (knowledge
2. Psychomotor (skill),
3. Affective (value)

Learning objectives should describe what students will know, be able to do, or be like as a result of your instruction. Break down your learning objectives to reflect the three domains and always use ACTION verbs:

Knowledge outcome: By the end of 45/35/20 minutes of teaching this lesson, my students will be able to:

- List all the items on a periodic table.
- Translate a paragraph of text from English to French.
- Apply basic web development skills to develop electronic portfolios.
- Diagnose learning disabilities in K–8 settings.

Skill outcome: By the end of 45/35/20 minutes of teaching this lesson, my students will be able to:

- Write a reflection paper.
- Perform CPR on a patient.
- Drive a car without adult supervision.
- Draw a chart to explain the data.

Affective outcome: By the end of 45/35/20 minutes of teaching this lesson, my students will be able to:

- Develop respect and tolerance of other people/cultures.
- Engage in constructive discussion of sensitive social and ethical issues.
- Engage in a social action activities to promote common good.
- Debate multiple sides of an argument.

Materials/Resources:
(*List materials and resources needed to teach this lesson.*)

Orchestration of Teaching

1. Checking Students' Prior Knowledge (2–3 minutes)
- You want to know how much students already know about the concept/topic/material you are introducing.

2. Introduction of the Learning Material. (1–2 minutes)
- Tell students what they are going to learn.
- Why it is important that they learn (relevance).
- How they are going to learn (in groups, independently, whole class, in a lab, or outside the classroom).
- Students are unpredictable but they expect you to be predictable. They want to know what comes next and why they need to do it. You can also write the agenda of the day on the side of the white board so they can see and follow what comes next.

3. Modeling (optional, depending on the nature of the lesson) (2 minutes)
- Demonstrate what you expect students to do before they get at it.

4. Engaging Students in Learning Experiences/Activities
- The number of activities students are engaged in should match and reflect the number of objectives you stated.
- Allocate more time to an activity you deem challenging; therefore, students might need more time to complete.
- Manage and monitor students' interactions with each other, answer their questions.
- Clarify your objectives and expectations.
- Move around when necessary to check and assess the learning progress.
- Anticipate difficulties a student/group may have during the completion of the activity. At the end of each activity, let students celebrate their accomplishment; find out what completing the activity meant to them; what the challenges were and what they have learned before taking them from the first activity to the next; help them make connections from their learning to the new learning in the subsequent activity.

LESSON PLANS

Activity # 1 (Name and describe the activity) *(3–5 minutes)*
Transition

Activity # 2 (Name and describe the activity) *(5–10 minutes)*

Transition

Activity # 3 (Name and describe the activity) *(10–15 minutes)*

Transition

5. Closure: Marking the end of the lesson and a sense of accomplishment for students (3–4 minutes)

- Tell students what you have taught and what they have learned or ask them randomly about what has been taught to them and what they have learned. Focus on the BIG IDEA.

The Integrated Unit Planning

There is no single format for a teaching unit that works best. Particular formats may be best for specific disciplines, topics, or grade levels. There is no set time period that a unit plan should cover. The exact time duration will be dictated by several factors, including the topic, the grade level, the interest, and abilities of your students. Plan a unit that meets the GLCEs for the strand you are teaching. Involve more than one discipline, such as science and math or social studies and language arts, or all four integrated throughout the unit. It enables students to learn by making connections among subjects in one single lesson.

Lesson Plan Template

There is no single lesson plan format to follow; this is just one format that you can use in this class. You can use other formats that suit your teaching style best. Each format has its own vocabulary. Whatever format you choose MUST contain at least the following steps.

Sample # 2

NAME_____ School_____

Curriculum Area_____ Grade level_____ Date _____

Lesson Title:

Teaching Goal(s): BIG IDEA or Purpose

GLCE(s):

Learning Objective(s): Learning objectives should describe what students should know, be able to do, or be like by the end of a lesson/unit. The learning objectives focus on different domains: cognitive (knowledge), psychomotor (skill), and affective (value). (See Bloom's action verb list)

Example of Knowledge outcome: By the end of this lesson, students will be able to:

    a. List all the items on a periodic table.
    b. Translate a paragraph of text from English to French .
    c. Apply basic web development skills to develop electronic portfolios.
    d. Diagnose learning disabilities in K–8 settings.

Example of Skill outcome: By the end of this lesson, students will be able to:

    a. Write a reflection paper.
    b. Perform CPR on a patient.
    c. Teach driving lessons to teens.
    d. Draw a chart to explain the data.

Example of Affective outcome: By the end of this lesson, students will be able to:

    a. Develop respect and tolerance of other people/cultures.
    b. Engage in constructive discussion of sensitive social and ethical issues.
    c. Engage in a social action activities to promote common good.
    d. Debate multiple sides of an argument.

Materials/resources:
(*List materials and resources needed to teach this lesson.*)

Delivery/Orchestration of Teaching

1. Checking students' prior knowledge (2–3 minutes)
- You want to know how much students already know about the concept/topic/material you are introducing.

2. Introduction of the learning material. (1–2 minutes) *Tell students what they are going to learn .*
- Why it is important that they learn (relevance)?

LESSON PLANS

- How they are going to learn (in groups, independently, whole class, in a lab, or outside the classroom)?
- Students are unpredictable but they expect you to be predictable. They want to know what comes next and why they need to do it. You can also write the agenda of the day on the side of the white board so they can see and follow what comes next.

3. Modeling *(optional, depending on the nature of the lesson)* *(2 minutes)*

- You want your students to see you demonstrate what you expect them to do before they get at it.

4. Engaging students in learning experiences/activities

- The number of activities students are engaged in should match and reflect the number of objectives stated.
- You allocate more time to an activity you deem challenging; therefore, students might need more time to complete.
- You manage and monitor students' interactions with each other, you answer their questions, you clarify your objectives and expectations, you move around when necessary to check and assess the learning progress, you anticipate difficulties a student/group may have during the completion of the activity.

Activity # 1 (Name and describe the activity) *(3–5 minutes)*

Transition (At the end of each activity let students celebrate their accomplishment; find out what completing the activity meant to them; the challenges and what they have learned before taking them from the first activity to the next; help them make connections of their learning to the new learning in the subsequent activity.

Activity # 2 (Name and describe the activity) *(5–10 minutes)*

Transition

Activity # 3 (Name and describe the activity) *(10–15 minutes)*

Transition

5. Closure/Conclusion: Marking the end of the lesson and a sense of accomplishment for students. *(3–4 minutes)*

- Tell students what you have taught and what they have learned or ask them randomly about what has been taught to them and what they have learned. Remind them of any homework you have for them and when it is due just before they leave your class.

LESSON PLANS

Sample Lesson Plan

Name: School: Springfield Plaines Elementary

Curriculum Area: Social Studies   Grade Level: 6th Grade

Date: Thursday, September 30, 2010

Lesson Title: The World in Spatial Terms

Teaching Goals: To teach an understanding of the countries around the United States and their location in the through the use of maps and current events.

GLCES: 6-GI.1.2 Draw a sketch map from memory showing the major region (Canada, United States, Mexico, Central America, South America, and Caribbean).

Learning Objectives:
- **Knowledge outcome:** By the end of this lesson, students will be able to:
  - Discuss each country in the western hemisphere in regards to location, surrounding countries and surrounding bodies of water.
  - Be familiar with countries in the western hemisphere.
  - Skill outcome: By the end of this lesson, students will be able to correctly label a map of the western hemisphere

- **Affective outcome:** By the end of this lesson, students will be able to:
  - Develop a respect and greater understanding for other countries in the western hemisphere.
  - Develop an appreciation for the United States.
  - Understand differences between the United States and other countries in the western hemisphere.

- **Materials:**
  - Paper
  - Colored pencils
  - Map of the western hemisphere
  - CNN News article: "1,000 people could be trapped in Mexico landslide, governor says."
  - Blown-up map of the western hemisphere
  - Individual cut-outs of countries (with Velcro) in the western hemisphere
  - Strips of paper including every country in the western hemisphere
  - A class set of unlabeled maps for the students to color and label individually
  - A class set of labeled maps
  - Unlabeled maps (one map for each set of partners for assessment)

Orchestration of Teaching

1. ***Checking students' prior knowledge:***
    -   Did anyone hear of the landslide that recently happened in Mexico?
    -   Does anyone know where Mexico is located?
    -   Where is Mexico in relationship to the United States? (I will have a map of the world and students will be able to come to the front of the class one at a time and show the class where Mexico is located.)

2. ***Introduction of the learning material:***
    In introducing the western hemisphere to the class, I will pass out the CNN article about the landslides in Oaxaca, Mexico. I will ask the students to read the current-event article and write down three things they notice about how life in Mexico is different from life in the United States. I will tell the students that over the next couple of days, we will be learning about the different countries that make up the western hemisphere. Students will be asked to color and label a map of the western hemisphere and memorize the location of the countries. Our world is a much bigger than just the United States and it is important that students be familiar with other countries' locations, cultures, and customs. Today, students will be coloring and labeling a map of the western hemisphere individually. Students will also be creating a Velcro map of the western hemisphere as a class. Lastly, students will work with partners to test their knowledge on the location of countries in the western hemisphere.

3. ***Modeling:***
    To model this lesson, I will show the students a sample colored map of the western hemisphere that I have created.
    -   Engage students in learning activity:

Activity #1. Making Maps (10 minutes)
In order to gain an understanding of the world around us, students will be creating maps of the western hemisphere. I will pass out to each student an outline of the countries included in the western hemisphere along with a labeled map of the western hemisphere. I will then ask the students to color each country a different color, and label each with its name. Students will also be asked to label the bodies of water that encompass the western hemisphere.

Activity #2. Velcro Map Activity (30 minutes)
To begin the next activity, I will show the students a large poster board of a blown-up map of the western hemisphere. I will have all of the countries that are included in the western hemisphere individually cut out. Each country will have a small piece of Velcro on the back of it, which will match up with a piece of Velcro on the large poster board map. I will have the name of each country on a slip of paper, and will put all the slips of paper in a paper bag. One at a time, students will draw the name of a country. As the student draws the name of a country, I will read students an interesting fact about that country. I will also show this fact on the visualizer or overhead projector for students to copy down in their notebooks. The student who drew the country from the bag will come to the front of the room and find the cut-out of this country.

The student will then match the country with its location on the large poster board map. This activity will continue until the map of the western hemisphere has been successfully created.

Activity #3. Partner Map Assessment (10 minutes)

To test the students' knowledge on how much information they retained from the previous activity, I will count the class off so that each person is partnered with one other classmate. I will then pass out an unlabeled map of the western hemisphere and ask for each set of partners to label the map to the best of its ability. Since the western hemisphere has just been introduced to the class, I will provide a word bank for this activity. Partners will be asked to complete this activity as thoroughly as possible. After they have completed this activity, I will pass out a correctly labeled map. Students will correct their own maps to see which countries they correctly labeled and which countries were mislabeled.

4. **Conclusion:**
   - Today we learned about various countries in the western hemisphere. Were you familiar with any of these countries before coming to class today? What did you learn that you did not already know about any country in the western hemisphere?
   - How can maps be helpful?
   - Why is it important to use maps to create an understanding of the world around us?
   - Tomorrow, we will again be testing our knowledge on the countries of the western hemisphere. By the end of this week, it will be expected that you know the location of each country in the western hemisphere. For homework, students should practice and study their maps tonight at home. I will also tell the students that on Monday they will be given a map of the western hemisphere that they must label correctly. This will be the end of the unit assessment.

LESSON PLANS

Developing a Social Studies Unit: Suggested Steps

There is no single format for a teaching unit that works best. Particular formats may be best for specific disciplines topics, or grade levels.

There is no set time period that a unit plan should cover.

The exact time duration will be dictated by several factors, including the topic, the grade level, the interest and abilities of your students, and your teaching style.

Select a unit that meets your teaching style and students' learning needs.

The Conventional Unit Plan

This plan is made of a series of lessons centered on a topic, theme, major concept, or block of subject matter (transportation, food, health, etc.) delivered during several days.

Each lesson builds on the lesson taught the previous day by contributing additional subject matter, providing further illustrations, and supplying more practice, all of which are aimed at bringing about mastery of the knowledge and skills on which the unit is centered.

The Integrated Unit Plan

More than one discipline, such as science and math or social studies and language arts, or all four, are integrated throughout the unit. It enables students to learn by making connections among subjects in one single lesson.

The Self-Instructional Unit

It is a unit that is designed for individualized self-instruction. It covers less content than the previous units and can be completed in an hour or less. It consists of instruction, references, exercises, problems, and all materials and information that a student needs to complete the task independently. You can have students work on the units individually at their own speed, and different students can work on different units at the same time. Students who successfully complete a unit can move to another unit without having to wait for other students to catch up. Such units help to assess the gradual progress of students in multiage or non-grade classrooms. You can use them for remediation, enrichment, or make-up purposes.

Steps
Step # 1. Select a theme from the NCSS list of themes and a concept from the core democratic values.

Step # 2. Check the grade-level content knowledge, skills, and values expectations for the given grade for which you are writing the unit and write a rationale for the unit plan you have selected.

Helpful hints you need to consider:

- Be familiar with the topic and materials.
- Consult the state frameworks; for example, the Michigan 7th Entry Level Standards
- Decide what content you want your students to learn, along with why and how.
- Write specific learning objectives; what you hope students will learn.
- Your objectives have to match the curriculum goals.
- Write the objectives in behavioral (performance) terms.
- Gather ideas from curriculum documents, libraries, peers, other teachers.

- Check the learning activities to make sure that they will actually contribute to your stated learning objectives.

Step # 3. Write clear and challenging learning activities.

- Can I afford the time, effort, expense?
- Do I have the necessary materials, equipment, or resources?
- If not, can they be obtained? Where, when, and how? You must plan long before the unit begins for media equipment and materials, references, reading materials, and community resources.
- Are the learning activities developmentally appropriate? In other words, are the activities suited to the intellectual and maturity levels of your students?

Step # 4. Decide how you are going to introduce the unit.

- Check students' prior knowledge.
- Provide introductory activities that stimulate students' interest.
- Inform students of the content of the unit.
- Know your students' (interests, abilities, experiences, and their present knowledge of the topic.
- Make transitions that bridge the topic with what the students have already learned.
- Involve students as much as possible. (Remember, you are not teaching them, you learn with and from them, too.) The more involved your students are, the less discipline problem you have in your class.

Step # 5. Manage and assess student learning.

- Plan to gather information in several ways:
  - Observe student performance
  - Question-Answer
  - Portfolio assessment
  - Paper and pencil assessment
- Assessment criteria must be consistent with specific learning objectives.

Step # 6. Closure:

- Plan culminating activities that:
  - Summarize what has been taught and what has been learned.
  - Provide transfer to the subsequent unit.

Unit Planning: Practice Exercise

Based on the information about developing a unit plan, select a topic, theme, or concept from each of the strands and develop an integrated teaching unit to be used at a grade level that your team agreed upon.

LESSON PLANS

Points to consider in evaluating a unit plan's exercise:

1. What type of unit is it? _____
2. Does it have a suggested duration? _____
3. Are the educational goals clearly stated? _____
   _____
4. Are learning objectives specific and clearly stated? _____
   _____
5. Are there appropriate questions leading to the achievement of the learning objectives? _____
   _____
6. Are teaching procedures clearly stated? _____
   _____
   _____
7. Do the learning activities appear feasible? _____
   _____
   _____
   _____
8. Does the unit have an introductory activity? _____
   _____
   _____
   _____
9. Does the plan include developmentally appropriate activities? _____
   _____
   _____
10. Does the plan include culminating activities? _____
11. Does the unit include learning assessment strategies?_____
12. Are the assessment strategies diagnostic, formative, or summative?
13. Does the unit identify the materials needed for implementation of the unit? Does it appear that the materials are readily available?
14. Does the unit take into account student differences in learning styles and abilities?
15. Identify the various teaching strategies used in this unit
16. Specifically where and how does this unit plan address the following?
    - Student reading skills_____
    - Student study skills_____
    - Student thinking skills_____
    - Student learning skills_____
17. Are there content-related activities to be studied in the unit?
18. Anything missing in this unit plan? What?
19. Will any student-teacher, teacher, and/or substitute teacher use and implement this unit plan successfully?

Evaluating a Lesson Plan

Instructions: The purpose of this exercise is to assess the effectiveness of your own lesson/unit plan. Based on your assessment, make changes as necessary. For each of the 21 items, you should write Yes/No and a brief comment.

1. Are adequate descriptive data provided?
2. Are teaching objectives clear and practical?
3. Is the rationale clear and justifiable?
4. Is the content appropriate for children at this grade level?
5. Does the content contribute to achievement of the objectives?
6. Is the plan workable given the time frame?
7. Does the plan engage students, motivating them to want to learn?
8. Does the plan indicate how guided practice will be provided for each child?
9. Are assignments clear, manageable, and related to the lesson objectives?
10. Is adequate closure provided to reinforce learning, convey a sense of completeness?
11. Are materials appropriate for the grade level and adequate to meet the needs of all students?
12. Does evaluative criteria provide informal data to determine how much students have learned from the lesson?
13. Does evaluative criteria provide formal data to determine how much students have learned from the lesson?
14. Is the lesson/unit plan in any way connected with other aspects of the curriculum to provide for integration of subject matter?
15. Does the lesson attend to the total child: emotionally, physically, cognitively, socially, morally, and ethically?
16. Does the lesson provide a sense of meaning for the students?
17. Is an adequate amount of time allotted to address the information presented?
18. Is there anything missing in this lesson/unit plan?
19. Could another student-teacher or substitute teacher follow and implement this plan easily?
20. Do grade level content expectations (GLCEs) match the strand and the learning activities?
21. Is the BIG IDEA clearly articulated in the plan?

To show that you have mastered instructional planning skills satisfactorily, you must score all 21 answers with a yes. If you marked fewer than 21 answers with a yes, it means that you need to work on those areas that you missed. As you review the questions and are thinking of what you need to change you are reflecting and making sense of what you are doing. You are learning to become a reflective practitioner.

LESSON PLANS

FURTHER TEXTS

Bring the World into the Classroom through Quality Children's Literature

The push to empower American children with twenty-first century skills demands that educators meet the federal, state, and local expectations for excellence. In order to meet these expectations, educators need to adopt strategies that require them to integrate grade-level content-specific standards into their lessons. They can do so by:

- Selecting high-quality trade books for use in the classroom.
- Combining children's literature with the National Council for Social Studies' "Thematic Strands." Chapter VI provides examples of high-quality children's literature that enhances learning of culture and global perspectives; an instrument for determining quality children's literature; and practical suggestions, strategies, and ideas on how to integrate literacy resources and social studies themes in creative and meaningful ways. The National Council for Social Studies (NCSS) developed ten thematic strands on which to base social studies instruction in K–12 classrooms.
- The process of selecting a high-quality trade book for a given grade and classroom requires that teachers examine literary elements including: the characterization, the plot, the theme, the setting, the style, and illustrations. Additionally, the book to be selected should be free of biases and stereotypes. The selection should include a variety of genres, and the book must match the selected social studies theme (Hilke, 1999).

For that purpose, an assessment inventory is needed.

Assessment Inventory

Another way to identify a high-quality book for teaching social studies elementary classrooms is using an assessment inventory to examine the literary elements in the book and determine if it should be recommended for use in the classroom.

When selecting a picture book for classroom use, a teacher must ensure that it is high-quality literature that will interest children. The process involves examining literary elements such as: theme, plot, setting, characterization, author's style, and illustrations, free of biases, stereotypes, and misrepresentation.

Fig. 1. An assessment inventory for selecting high quality children's picture books to teach social studies themes. Adapted from Deborah A. Mayer, Checklist for choosing children's literature to teach science, Science and Children, March 1995, 18.

Title of Book: _____   Author_____

1. Theme
   a. What is the Big Idea?
   b. What is the social studies concept that children would learn?
   c. In which social studies strand does the concept belong? History/Economics/Geography/ Civic Engagement/Public Discourse.

2. Storyline
   a. Which strategy does the author use?
      - Inquiry
      - Primary sources
      - Narrative
   b. Does the story allow children to distinguish fact from fiction?

3. Characters
   a. Are characters in the story depicted naturally?
   b. Are characters believable?

4. Setting
   a. Does the story take place in a realistic setting?
   b. Are time relationships appropriate?

5. Style
   a. Which plot structure does the story use?

6. Illustrations
   a. Do the illustrations portray accurate cultural representations?
   b. Do the illustrations match the story?

7. Stereotyping
   a. Are any stereotypes present?

8. Misrepresentations
   a. Are there misrepresentations that could lead to stereotyping and bias?

Recommendation (circle one)

High-quality picture book   Medium quality   Poor quality

Selected Social Studies Themes

Students read a wide range of print and non-print texts to build an understanding of themselves, and of the cultures of the United States and the world; to acquire new information; to respond to the needs and demands of society and the workplace; and for personal fulfillment. Among these texts are fiction and nonfiction, classic and contemporary works.

Students read a wide range of literature from many periods in many genres to build an understanding of the many dimensions (e.g., philosophical, ethical, aesthetic) of human experience.

Students apply a wide range of strategies to comprehend, interpret, evaluate, and appreciate texts. They draw on their prior experience, their interactions with other readers and writers, their knowledge of word meaning and of other texts, their word identification strategies, and their understanding of textual features (e.g., sound-letter correspondence, sentence structure, context, graphics).

Much More Social Studies Through Children's Literature: A Collaborative Approach

When Africa Was Home

Author: Karen Lynn Williams, Illustrator: Floyd Cooper, Publisher: Orchard Books, Year: 1991.
Social Studies Theme: Culture

The anthills of Africa were taller than Peter—at least when he was little and Africa was home. His playmates in the village didn't think a thing about his white skin or golden hair. But his nanny did. Mayi told Peter's mother the boy should wear a hat because of the hot sun. Somehow, Peter never wore a hat in Africa. He ran up the anthills barefoot and ate sugar cane in the shade of red flame trees. But when Peter has to return to his home in America, he misses Africa deeply. He misses his friend, Yekha, and his Mayi. He misses hearing the hippos moo, the hyenas groan, and the drums sing in the distance. More than anything he wishes he were home again in Africa. The book's eloquent words and glowing pictures show why.

Sundiata

Author and Illustrator: David Wisniewski, Publisher: Clarion Books, 1992.
Social Studies Theme: Culture

The story of Sundiata, son of the King of Mali in the time of the great trading empire of Africa some eight hundred years ago, is a powerful tale of courage and determination. As a boy, Sundiata was unable to speak or walk. He overcame these obstacles, but was driven into exile by a rival queen, Sassourna Berete, when his father, King Maghan Kon Fatta, begins to prepare him for his place on the throne. When Mali was overrun by the forces of a sorcerer king, the 18-year-old Sundiata returned to defeat the intruder and claim the throne.

The Day Gogo Went to Vote

Author: Elinor Batezat Sisulu, Illustrator: Sharon Wilson, Publisher: Little, Brown, & Company, Year: 1996. **Social Studies Theme: Culture**

Thembi, the ingenuous six-year-old narrator, describes how her 100-year-old great-grandmother, Gogo, makes the long trip to the polls to cast her vote during South Africa's 1994 democratic elections, the first in which blacks were allowed to vote. When she first announces her plans, the family is shocked, because Gogo is too frail to leave the yard. "You want me to die not having voted?" Gogo asks Thembi's anxious parents. The oldest voter in the township, Gogo emerges from the voting booth to the sound of applause and the glare of camera flashes, and the reader, too, will feel the momentousness of the occasion and the characters' jubilation.

Bonyo Bonyo

Author: Vanita Oelnschlager, Illustrators: Kristin Blackwood and Mike Elanc,
Publisher: VanitaBooks, Year: 2010. **Social Studies Theme: Culture**

When he was a child, Bonyo Bonyo's baby sister died. That sad event was the start of a hopeful dream: someday he would build a hospital in his village in western Kenya. This first-person picture book narrative tells how young Bonyo was able to fulfill that dream through education obtained with steadfast support from his family despite the sacrifices required, and countless other acts of generosity and kindness. "In my village there was a word that meant togetherness. That word was 'harambee.' I will never forget how everyone helped me." Bonyo attended medical school in Akron, Ohio (where he practices medicine today), and was able to return to Kenya 15 years after leaving and turn his dream into a reality. He established a medical mission and a clinic in his home village named in honor of his mother.

Silent Music

Author: James Rumford, Publisher: A Neal Porter Book/Roaring Brook Press, Year: 2008.
Social Studies Theme: Culture

Ali lives in Baghdad and is passionate about learning to write Arabic. For him the calligraphy is not just about communication but also the beauty of the characters and what they represent. He likes other things, too, especially soccer, but the letters are what he loves most of all. "Writing a long sentence is like watching a soccer player in slow motion as he kicks the ball across the field, as I leave a trail of dots and loops behind me." Ali's hero is Yakut, a famous calligrapher who lived in Baghdad 800 years ago. Then, as now, there was a war in Baghdad. And like Yakut, Ali writes to "fill my mind with peace."

Babu's Song

Author: Stephanie Stuve-Bodeen, Illustrator: Aaron Boyd, Publisher: Lee & Low, Year: 2007.
Social Studies Theme: Culture

Bernardi would love to go to school, but he and his grandfather, Babu don't have enough money to pay the fees. Bernardi would also love a soccer ball, but the one he has seen in the store costs more than the fees for school. One day Babu makes Bernardi a music box that plays the same tune the elderly man used to sing before he lost his voice to an illness. Bernardi loves hearing the song again, but in the marketplace where he sells the toys Babu makes, a persistent tourist pressures him into selling the box. He now has enough money to buy the soccer ball. He also has a broken heart, wishing he'd kept his grandfather's gift. Stephanie Stuve-Bodeen's story about a contemporary Tanzanian child, Bernardi, relates feelings that all children can identify with in any setting.

Time to Pray
Author: MahaAddasi, Illustrator: Ned Gannon, Publisher: Boyds Mills Press, Year: 2010.
Social Studies Theme: Culture

"Come to pray, come to pray," calls the muezzin in the middle of the night, waking young Yasmin during her stay with her grandmother in the Middle East. It's a call that resonates with Yasmin, and her grandmother, Teta, helps her begin her spiritual practice. She takes Yasmin to the fabric store and purchases cloth for prayer clothes, helps her select a special prayer rug, and finally demonstrates how to wash before praying. Then Yasmin makes her first trip to the mosque to pray with Teta. The phrase "time to pray" takes on several meanings, not only reflecting Yasmin's start of her intentional spiritual practice but also the call of the muezzin.

Kali and the Rat Snake
Author: Zai Whitaker, Illustrator: Srividya Natarajan, Publisher: Kane/Miller Books, Year: 2006.
Social Studies Theme: Culture

Kali's father is a snake catcher—the best in the village in Southern India. Kali knows that is really something to be proud of, for he is one of the Irula, an indigenous tribal people. But at school he sometimes gets embarrassed. The other children seem to think there is something very strange about having a snake catcher for a father and eating things like fried termites for a snack. Plus, Kali is the teacher's pet. How will he ever make friends?

The Bracelet
Author: Yoshiko Uchida, Illustrator: Joanna Yardley, Publisher: Philomel, Year: 1993.
Social Studies Theme: Time, Change, and Continuity

The author wrote this story based on her experience in an internment program in World War II. Before Emi, a young Japanese American child, and her family leave for the relocation center at Tanforan, her Caucasian friend, Laurie, gives her a bracelet as a symbol of their friendship. When Emi reaches the filthy horse stall that will be her home, she notices the loss of the bracelet. At first she is devastated and certain that she has lost her friend too, but she soon discovers that her memories will always remain in her heart.

Children of the Dust Bowl

Author: Jerry Stanley, Publisher: Crown, Year: 1995.
Social Studies Theme: Time, Change & Continuity

This book tells the stories of children of Oklahoma families who migrated to California in the 1930s and 40s. It begins with poignant, vivid, and unforgettable descriptions of the hopelessness of their lives before, during, and after their arrival. One person writes of running out of food en route to California. The kids waited for the adults to share the coffee and then took up spoons to eat the coffee grounds. Beaten down by starvation, disease, and widespread prejudice, the children turn despair around by building their own school. Ownership and pride give them hope. In the words of one student, "This is what we are now, but it's not what we're going to be." And for most of them, this prophecy proved true. Photo and journalistic documentation combine with a powerful writing style to make this an inspiring, nonfiction read-aloud.

The Middle Passage

Author and Illustrator: Tom Feelings, Publisher: Dial, Year: 1995.
Social Studies Theme: Time, Change & Continuity

This beautiful wordless book captures the silent scream of Africans on their way to the institution of slavery. The book begins when the author fled the sadness of 1960s Civil Rights America to find the joys of Africa. While working in Ghana, he was asked, "What happened to all of you when you were taken away from here?" Answers came to him in bits and pieces over the next 30 years. As Feelings describes the horrific passage of African slaves en route to slavery in his 64 narrative paintings, he also speaks of his own journeys, the journeys of those he knows, has known, and never knew. Using pen and ink and tempera on rice paper, Tom Feelings hauntingly captures the pain of enslaved Africans as they journeyed through the middle passage from Africa to America. The muted colors express the story of the Africans' loss of freedom. The wordless plot includes the attack, capture, forced march, branding, life in the ship's hold, death at sea, and auction on land. The power of the book lies in its silence.

Pink and Say

Author & Illustrator: Patricia Polacco, Publisher: Philomel, Year: 1995.
Social Studies Theme: Time, Change & Continuity

While attempting to escape his unit after being wounded in the Civil War, Say is rescued by Pink, who carries him back to his Georgia home. Pink and his family had been slaves. After Say tells Pink and his mother that he once shook the hand of Abraham Lincoln, he reaches for Pink's hand and exclaims, "Now you can say you touched the hand that shook the hand of Abraham Lincoln!" Both boys are taken prisoners by the Confederate Army, and when the boys are separated, Pink reaches to touch Say's hand one last time. Say survives and was able to pass along the story to his daughter, Rosa, who was Patricia Polacco's great-grandmother. Pink was hanged shortly after being taken prisoner. At the end of the story,

FURTHER TEXTS

Patricia bids the reader, "Before you put this book down, say his name (Pinkus Aylee) out loud and vow to remember him always."

The Whispering Cloth

Author: Pegi Deitz Shea, Illustrators: Anita Riggio/You Yang, Publisher: Caroline House/Boyds Mills Press, Year: 1995. **Social Studies Theme: Time, Change & Continuity**

Mai, a young Hmong girl living in a refugee camp in Thailand, waits for the day she might join her cousins in the United States. To pass time, Mai listens to the women tell stories of their Laotian homeland and she watches the stories take shape inside the beautiful borders of the pa'ndau, the story cloth they sew. Wanting to stitch her own pa'ndau, Mai finds herself remembering the death of her parents and her flight from Laos to the refugee camp with her grandmother.

My Freedom Trip

Authors: Frances Park and Ginger Park, Illustrator: Debra Reid Jenkins, Publisher: Boyd Mills Press, Year: 1998. **Social Studies Theme: Time, Change & Continuity**

A young girl describes her journey from North to South Korea in this haunting picture book that reveals a small child's fear of leaving what is loved and familiar behind and of journeying into the unknown. Soo's friends have already been disappearing one by one from school, fleeing with their families in the night to the freedom of the south on the eve of the Korean War. When her father tells her that he, too, will be leaving, Soo begs him to stay but he promises her his guide, Mr. Han, will return for her soon, and then for her mother. One by one, he tells her, they will take their freedom trips. When the guide does return for Soo, she must go with this kind stranger into the night, leaving her mother behind and trusting that her father will be waiting at the end of her journey. The authors based the unforgettable story on their own mother's childhood. Their prose is as hushed and tense as a child in fear as Soo and Mr. Han move through the dangerous darkness, and Debra Reid Jenkins' soft, somber-toned paintings underscore the emotional weight of the story. A key is provided to the Korean words used in the text and the Korean characters that appear as part of the design of each quiet, elegant two-page spread.

The Butterfly

Author and Illustrator: Patricia Polacco, Publisher: Philomel, Year: 2000.
Social Studies Theme: Time, Change & Continuity

Once again, readers are introduced to members of the author's extended family. The setting is in a small village in France during the Nazi occupation during World War II. Her great aunt Marcel Solliliage and her daughter Monique became a part of the French Resistance. What young Monique first thinks is a ghost in her room turns out to be a young Jewish girl, Severine, being hidden with her parents in Monique's basement. The girls steal moments of pleasure together but unfortunately, they were seen by a neighbor and had to flee. The story is filled with tension, symbolism, and the brutality of occupation. The mistreatment of the Jews is not whitewashed. As the author's note reveals, only the daughter survived. *This picture book is for older readers because it requires an understanding of World War II and the persecution of the Jews.*

The Yellow Star

Author: Carmen Agra Deedy, lllustrator: Henri Sorenson, Publisher: Peachtree, Year: 2000.
Social Studies Theme: Time, Change & Continuity

"Early in the year 1940, in the country of Denmark, there were only Danes. Tall Danes. Short Danes. Old Danes. Silly Danes. Cranky Danes ... and even some Great Danes. But no matter how different from each other they seemed, the Danes held one thing in common. All were loyal subjects of their beloved King Christian." At one point during the World War II occupation of Denmark, the Nazis required all Jews to identify themselves by wearing a yellow Star of David on their outer clothes. The legend retold here is one in which the King risks everything—his identity, his monarchy, and his very life in an attempt to stop the Nazis from tearing apart his country and harming his people. As a model of righteousness, as a clever strategist, and as a devoted leader, King Christian X sets the standard. The king appeared unescorted in public the next day wearing a yellow star. Other Gentiles were inspired to wear yellow stars, too, and so the Nazi edict lost its frightful power. Deedy lists documented facts and points out a universal truth in the legend.

A Hero and the Holocaust: The Story of Janusz Korczak and His Children

Author: David A. Adler, Illustrator: Bill Farnsworth, Publisher: Holiday House, Year: 2002.
Social Studies Theme: Time, Change & Continuity

David A. Adler adroitly manages to introduce readers to a complex person living in nearly incomprehensible times. As a young man in Warsaw, Henryk Goldszmit took the pen name Janusz Korczak to hide the fact that he was Jewish. After receiving his medical degree and working in a children's hospital, Korczak became the Director of a Jewish orphans' home. He became so committed to the children that he refused to leave them after the wall was built around the Warsaw Ghetto, or later as they were all herded onto the train that would take them to Treblinka and certain death. Adler's straightforward declarative sentences are accompanied by dramatic oil paintings of Korczak with the children.

Ruby's Wish

Author: Shirin Yim Bridges, Illustrator: Sophie Blackall, Publisher: Chronicle, Year: 2002.
Social Studies Theme: Time, Change & Continuity

Young Ruby loves the color red and she loves to learn. Living in China at a time when few girls were taught to read or write, Ruby eagerly studies with the tutors her grandfather has hired for any child in his house who wants to learn. Ruby excels, and her grandfather takes great pleasure in her success. So he's saddened and puzzled when he reads a poem Ruby has written lamenting her fate as a girl in a house "where only boys are cared for." Ruby's dream is to attend university—an option open to her boy cousins, but not to girls in China. Shirin Yin Bridges based this charming and ultimately uplifting story on the life of her grandmother, who, like the fictional Ruby, was accepted as one of the first female students at a university in China.

Circle Unbroken

Author: Margot Theis Raven, Illustrated by: E. B. Lewis, Publisher: Melanie Kroupa Books/Farrar, Straus and Giroux, Year: 2004. **Social Studies Theme: Time, Change & Continuity**

A grandmother connects the past with the present for her granddaughter as she teaches her how to make a sweetgrass basket. In doing so, she is bestowing two gifts on the child: the skill of basket weaving and the story of her past, which stretches back many generations to Africa. This story briefly but powerfully traces the history of African Americans through the child's family history, chronicling kidnappers in Africa and slavery in the United States, the Civil War and new hope, changing times and new challenges. Through it all, there are two constants: the passing of the skilled tradition and the love of parents and elders for children—always affirmed, just as the grandmother affirms her grandchild in many ways. The unbroken circle that the basket represents embraces the past and present, weaving them into the future. An author's note provides additional information about sweetgrass or "Gullah" baskets from the coastal islands off of South Carolina, where the story is set.

The Firekeeper's Son

Author: Linda Sue Park, Illustrator: Julia Downing, Publisher: Clarion, Year: 2004.
Social Studies Theme: Time, Change & Continuity

Sang-hee's father plays a vital role in their Korean village near the sea. As firekeeper, he climbs to the top of the mountain each evening to light a large bonfire. When the flames are visible on the next mountain, the firekeeper there lights his bonfire. When the king sees the fire on the mountain nearest the palace, he knows that the land is safe, and that no enemies have been seen approaching by sea. As long as the fires burn, the king will not send his soldiers to Sang-hee's village to defend the border. But when the fire is unlit one evening, and his father lies injured with a broken ankle and unable to climb the mountain, Sang-hee thinks how thrilling it would be if the soldiers came. Then, remembering his father's words about the value of peace, Sang-hee lets go of his fantasy and lights the signal fire himself. This engaging story set in the early 1800s is based on the bonfire signal system used in Korea until the late nineteenth century. Sang-hee's understandable desire for excitement is balanced with a welcome portrayal of heroic behavior during peaceful times.

The Greatest Skating Race

Author: Louise Borden, Illustrator: Niki Daly, Publisher: Margaret K. McElderry Books, Year: 2004.
Social Studies Theme: Time, Change & Continuity

A story set in 1941 takes place in the Netherlands, where young Piet dreams of being a great skater like his hero Pim Mulier of historic Elfstedentocht race fame. Piet's father is away fighting in World War II, but the very real dangers of that war are not just on far-off battlefields. Piet's country is occupied by the Germans, and when a classmate's father is arrested for owning a radio, Piet is asked to lead her and her younger brother to safety in a town in Belgium, 16 kilometers away. Piet, Johanna, and Joop must skate along the canals under the eyes of the Germans, acting as if they are just children at play. Johanna is a superb skater and Piet doesn't worry about her keeping up, but it's a struggle for young Joop. There are several tense moments made all the more difficult by the children's growing exhaustion as they stride toward the journey's conclusion in Louise Borden's dramatic story.

The Flag With Fifty-Six Stars

Author: Susan Goldman Rubin, Illustrator: Bill Farnsworth Publisher: Holiday House, Year: 2005.
Social Studies Theme: Time, Change & Continuity

In early May of 1945, SS guards began fleeing Mauthausen, a Nazi concentration camp in Austria. The starving prisoners knew the Americans must be near, and a small group of them began working on a surprise for their liberators. They took white from sheets, red from Nazi banners, and blue from their own tattered jackets. They located a sewing machine and scavenged needles and thread. When Colonel Richard R. Seibel of the American forces entered Mauthausen on May 6, he was presented with their gift: an American flag. The prisoners hadn't been certain how many stars to put on the flag, so they settled on 56. Susan Goldman Rubin did extensive research to write this moving, detailed account. In an author's note she indicates what is known for certain and what is still debated about the liberation of Mauthausen and the creation of the flag, which now is held at the Simon Wiesenthal Center in Los Angeles. A photograph of the flag at the end of Rubin's narrative serves as a tangible reminder of how the human spirit can endure, as long as there is hope.

The Librarian of Basra: A True Story From Iraq

Author: Jeanette Winter, Publisher: Harcourt, Year: 2005.
Social Studies Theme: Time, Change & Continuity

Alia Muhammad Baker is the librarian of Basra, Iraq. "Her library is a meeting place for all who love books. They discuss matters of the world and matters of the spirit. Until now—now they talk only of war." When the war reached Basra and bombs began to fall, Alia frantically called upon nearby neighbors of the library to help her save books while buildings in the city burned. Over the course of one night, they packed books in crates, sacks, and curtains, passing them over a seven-foot wall to hide them in the restaurant next door. In all, they saved 30,000 volumes, which Alia later hid in her own house and the houses of friends. There they remain, while Alia dreams of peace and a new library for Basra. The real-life, heroic efforts of Alia and others to save the books of Basra's library combines a tense, spare, present-tense narrative with stirring visual images that suggest the panic, destruction, and despair of war, but always in the context of the hope that grows from the actions and dreams of individuals determined to make a positive difference.

FURTHER TEXTS

The Wall

Author and Illustrator: Peter Sis, Publisher: Frances Foster Books/Farrar, Straus and Giroux, Year: 2007. **Social Studies Theme: Culture**

Peter Sis was born in Communist-controlled Brno, Czechoslovakia in 1949 and displayed artistic interests from very early on. His talents were indulged and encouraged within his home. At the same time, creativity and freedom of thought were being repressed in his school and throughout his homeland as the Iron Curtain rose and the Cold War escalated. Sis beautifully outlines the tension between socio-political repression and creativity through journal excerpts, actual drawings from his developing years as an artist, and hauntingly complex images outlining the historical context of turbulent times in Eastern Europe. Each image underscores how he questioned the world around him as a developing child and adolescent, especially as news of Western popular culture filtered through the curtain. Creative expression and opportunity exploded for the author in the spring of 1968, only to be crushed quickly by the totalitarianism's strong arm. Sis was able to hold onto his dreams, however, fueled by his indomitable spirit and the force of his own imagination.

Shin-chi's Canoe

Author: Nicola I. Campbell, Illustrator: Kim LaFave, Publisher: GroundwoodBooks/House Anansi Press, Year: 2008. **Social Studies Theme: Time, Change & Continuity**

Details of the Indian boarding school experience of Native children in the United States and in Canada, where this story is set, are the focus for this picture book. Forced by law to leave home to attend government-run schools where their language and culture are suppressed, siblings Shi-shi-etko (called Mary at school) and Shin-chi (David) are not allowed to speak to one another, so strict are the rules and so regimented the hours of their day. When he can bear missing his family no longer, Shin-chi sends the tiny carved canoe his father gave him down the river toward home. He knows he and Shi-shi-etko will follow when the school year finally ends. Days turn into weeks, and then months. There are bright spots, like Shin-chi's new friend, John. But the brightest of all is when June arrives—he and Shi-shi-etko are homeward bound at last.

Yuki and the One Thousand Carriers

Author: Gloria Whelan, Illustrator: Yan Nascimbene, Publisher: Sleeping Bear Press, Year: 2008. **Social Studies Theme: Time, Change & Continuity**

Gloria Whelan's "Yuki and the One Thousand Carriers" is the charming story of a little girl's reluctant but cushy trip by palanquin from her Kyoto home to Edo, now Tokyo. Yuki's father, a high-ranking provincial official, has a thousand serfs to transport his family and their belongings for their half-year stay in the shogunate capital. As she and her little dog, Kita, ride along with her mother in their silk-lined "wooden box," Yuki can look through the privacy shutters and see, far ahead, her father on horseback, leading their dragon-like procession. Yuki and Kita take breaks to scamper in the grass, and throughout the text Yuki's haiku commemorate her journey—and her homesickness—as she fulfills her teacher's request that she keep up her fledgling literary practice.

The Grand Mosque of Paris: A Story of How Muslims Rescued Jews During the Holocaust

Authors: Karen Gray Ruelle and Deborah Durland DeSaix, Publisher: Holiday House, Year: 2009.
Social Studies Theme: Time, Change & Continuity

An intriguing look at one setting in which some of the dramas of World War II played out is not only a fascinating dimension of history, but one that can broaden children's understanding of historical relations between Jews and Muslims. When the Germans occupied Paris during the war, some Jews in the city found refuge within the walls of the Grand Mosque of Paris. This enclave was the heart of the Muslim community in France. Under the leadership of Si Kaddour Benghabrit, rector of the mosque, members of the community, some of whom were part of the French Resistance, hid Jewish men, women, and children until they could get them safely out of the city.

Nasreen's Secret School: A True Story from Afghanistan

Author: Jeanette Winter, Publisher: Beach Lane, Year: 2009.
Social Studies Theme: Time, Change & Continuity

Based on a true story, Nasreen's tale opens with an author's note that details some of the changes in Afghanistan during the Taliban reign of 1996–2001, including the restriction on girls from attending school or university. Brave "citizens defied the Taliban in many ways, including supporting the secret schools for girls" both during and after the Taliban's control of Afghanistan. In the story, Nasreen lives alone with her grandmother after her father is seized by soldiers and her mother leaves to search for him. Nasreen does not speak after her parents' disappearance, and her grandmother decides to send her to a secret school for girls, hoping that she will "learn about the world ... and speak again." Although her silence persists for a long time, eventually Nasreen begins to talk to another girl at the school and learns to read, write, and do math. "Windows opened for Nasreen in that little schoolroom ... Nasreen no longer feels alone. The knowledge she holds inside will always be with her, like a good friend."

Benno and the Night of Broken Glass

Author: Meg Wiviott, Illustrator: Josee Bisaillon, Publisher: Kar-Ben, Year: 2010.
Social Studies Theme: Time, Change & Continuity

Benno the cat lives at Number 5 Rosenstrasse, where many people in the building care for him. Hans Hausmeister gives him fresh milk. Sophie Adler gives him chicken scraps after her family's Sabbath meal on Fridays. Inge Schmidt sneaks him schnitzel after church on Sundays. But Benno no longer sees Sophie and Inge walk to school together after "men in brown shirts" light a bonfire on the street one night. Soon, once-friendly faces yell, "Scat!" and people walk with lowered eyes as Benno tries to avoid the heavy boots of the brown-shirted men on the street. "Then came a night like no other ... At Moshe's butcher shop, they overturned the refrigerators ... Benno saw the beautiful neue Synagogue set ablaze ..." Meg Wiviott's remarkable narrative conveys the hugeness and inexplicable tragedy of events in 1938 Berlin from a neutral observer's perspective. An afterword provides more information on Kristallnacht, including photographs and a bibliography.

Half Spoon of Rice: A Survival Story of the Cambodian Genocide

Author: Icy Smith, Illustrator: Sopaul Nhem, Publisher: EastWest Discovery Press, Year: 2010.
Social Studies Theme: Time, Change & Continuity

Nat is a young boy in the midst of preparing for the Cambodian New Year celebration when sudden gunfire in the streets marks the start of terrible times. Along with thousands of others, Nat and his parents are forced out of the city by Khmer Rouge soldiers. Separated from his parents at a labor camp after days of walking, Nat spends the next four years fighting to survive as he works in the rice field. Troops from the Vietnamese Liberation Army eventually liberate the camp, and Nat and his friend, Malis, make their way over the border into Thailand, where Nat finds his parents. Malis is unable to learn the fate of her own family. Nat's voice is matter-of-fact yet full of feeling in a narrative that is honest about the horror and pain but never overwhelms with explicit details in a story that concludes with Nat's family about to emigrate to the United States. An extensive author's note provides more information about the Cambodian genocide in the 1970s, including photographs of child laborers.

Sitti's Secrets

Author: Naomi Shihab Nye, Illustrator: Nancy Carpenter, Publisher: Four Winds Press, Year: 1994.
Social Studies Theme: Global Connections

Mona's grandmother, Sitti. lives "on the other side of the earth" in a Palestinian village on the West Bank. Despite their uncommon language, she and her grandmother share daily life and special moments together when Mona and her father take a trip to visit Sitti. Upon her return to the United States, Mona writes a letter to the president: "If the people of the United States could meet Sitti, they'd like her for sure. You'd like her, too." Paired with Nancy Carpenter's sun-drenched illustrations, Naomi Shihab Nye's poetic text explores a child's feelings and fears about a grandparent living far away in a part of the world that most children in the United States know only one-dimensionally, if at all, through reports in the news

Only a Pigeon

Authors: Jane and Christopher Kurtz, Illustrator: E B. Lewis, Publisher: Simon & Schuster, Year: 1997.
Social Studies Theme: Global Connections

Ondu-ahlem goes to school every morning and spends his afternoons shining shoes in the market area to earn some spending money. Busy as he is, his thoughts are never far from the homing pigeons he is raising. He spends most of his free time caring for them—checking on the eggs that are just about ready to hatch and protecting them from the pesky mongoose who visits frequently at night. Inspired by the experiences of a real boy Jane and Christopher Kurtz met in Addis Ababa, Ethiopia, the story captures the child's deep devotion to his pigeons. E.B. Lewis's rich water color illustrations shimmer with small details of Ondu-ahlem's everyday life.

My Rows and Piles of Coins

Author: Tololwa M. Mollel, Illustrator: E.B. Lewis, Publisher: Clarion Books, Year: 1999.
Social Studies Theme: Global Connections

Set in a Tanzanian village in the early 1960s, this compelling story is based on a memory from the author's own childhood. Young Saruni has always helped his parents in the marketplace and they have frequently rewarded him with a ten-cent piece. What his parents don't know is that Saruni is secretly saving all his coins so that he may one day buy a bicycle to be even more help to his parents. Cultural details come through both in E.B. Lewis' sun-dappled watercolor illustrations and in the story itself, as we see the busy marketplace and realize that Saruni proudly contributes to his family's economic well-being. His strong desire to earn his own money to save up for something special, however, will certainly strike a chord of recognition with children in the United States today.

Tea with Milk

Author and Illustrator: Allen Say, Publisher: Houghton Mifflin, Year: 1999.
Social Studies Theme: Global Connections

The author provides a glimpse into his family through the eyes of his mother. Masako has never known her parents' homeland. She spent her life growing up in the United States. Just as she is planning to head off to college, the family returns to Japan. How frustrating—she is an outsider who must wear kimonos, sit on the floor, and worst of all, her parents have hired a matchmaker to find her a respectable husband. Masako rebelled at a time when properly raised girls in Japan just didn't leave home, head for the city, and look for a job. May, as she preferred to be called, found work in a department store where she also met her future husband, another foreigner who was raised by an English family. They discovered that they both share a love of tea with milk and sugar along with a desire to create their own home and place in the world.

The Composition

Author: Antonio Skarmeta, Illustrator: Alfonso Ruano, Publisher: A Groundwood Book/
Douglas A McIntyre, Year: 2000. **Social Studies Theme: Global Connections**

Chilean author Antonio Skarmeta's chilling short story about a nine-year-old boy growing up in a military dictatorship will provide plenty of food for thought. Pedro is an ordinary kid who likes to play soccer and wishes his parents would buy him a real soccer ball. He doesn't understand why his parents spend so much time huddled around the radio listening to news until his best friend's father is taken away by soldiers. For the first time, Pedro begins to understand the political implications of his parents' actions. "Am I against the dictatorship?" he asks his mother. "Children aren't against anything," she tells him. "Children are just children." When an army captain shows up at Pedro's school and demands that the students write a composition entitled, "What My Family Does at Night," Pedro does his best, hoping he will win a prize that will allow him to buy the soccer ball he wants so badly. Suspense builds throughout the story, right up until the final line of text, which packs quite a punch. A note at the end of the book helps to put the story into a broader context by describing some of the challenges faced by people living under a dictatorship where children are rewarded for turning on their parents.

FURTHER TEXTS

Snow in Jerusalem

Author: Deborah da Costa, Illustrators: Cornelius Van Wright and Ying-Hwa Hu,
Publisher: Albert A. Whitman, Year: 2001. **Social Studies Theme: Global Connections**

The Jewish boy Avi and the Muslim boy Hamudi don't know each other at the opening of this story set in the walled Old City of contemporary Jerusalem. But each boy knows and loves the beautiful white stray cat that comes to visit him regularly. When the cat doesn't show up for awhile, each boy becomes worried and goes in search of her through the ancient, ethnically diverse city, and that is how they meet. Once they find the cat, each boy wants to keep her for himself. But when they discover she has kittens and realize the free-spirited cat likes them both, they work out a peaceful resolution that suggests a future friendship. An author's note provides brief additional information on the history of Jerusalem and its diverse populations today. The full-color illustrations were created with watercolor and pencil.

Armando and the Blue Tarp School

Authors: Edith Hope Fine and Judith Pinkerton Josephson, Illustrator: Hernan Sosa,
Publisher: Lee & Low, Year: 2007. **Social Studies Theme: Global Connections**

For the children living in a colonia near a large city dump, school is held on a blue tarp spread on the ground. Teacher Senor David tells Armando and his friends that a school can be anywhere, and the children sit on the tarp as they study reading and math, sing songs, and play games. Armando must work beside his father at the dump, searching for discarded items to sell or use, and he wonders what he is missing at the blue tarp school. When his parents tell him that "learning is important," he is thrilled to leave the dump early each day to return to Senor David's classroom. The colonia is devastated when a fire sweeps through the dump, but the resulting newspaper article triggers a donation of money to build a school, and the blue tarp is exchanged for a small building with books and supplies. An informative authors' note tells of this fictional story's real-life inspiration: David Lynch's school for children in a colonia of the Tijuana city dump.

Four Feet, Two Sandals

Authors: Karen Lynn Williams and Khadra Mohammed, Illustrator: Doug Chayka,
Publisher: Eerdmans, Year: 2007. **Social Studies Theme: Global Connections**

A truck comes to the refugee camp where ten-year-old Lina lives with her mother and baby brothers on the Afghanistan-Pakistan border. From the truck, relief workers throw clothing to the crowd. Lina, who has gone barefoot for two years, is delighted to discover a yellow sandal adorned with a blue flower. It fits her foot perfectly. Looking up, she sees a girl her age with the other sandal. The two girls work out a comprise: "You wear them both today and I will wear them tomorrow." As the young girls take turns with the sandals, they share the stories that brought them both to the camp. When Lina finds out that her family is on the list to go to America, the girls find a way to keep their friendship—and the pair of

FURTHER TEXTS

sandals—unbroken, in a moving story that brings life in one small corner of the world into fuller relief for readers here.

The Wakame Gatherers

Author: Holly Thompson, Illustrator: Kazumi Wilds, Publisher: Shell's Books, Year: 2007.
Social Studies Theme: Global Connections

Nanami has two grandmothers: Gram, who lives in Maine, and Baachan, who lives with Nanami's family in Japan. Both live in seaside towns, but neither woman speaks the other's language. While Gram is visiting, Nanami acts as translator on an outing to collect wakame seaweed. For Nanami, a moment of child-like delight, as she asks Bachaan about gathering wakame when she was a child, turns into one of painful understanding: once, when they were young, her two grandmothers were on opposite sides of a war, one in which American bombs left Baachan motherless. But the pain is transcended by the obvious bond that the two women now share in their mutual respect and appreciation for nature and their love for their granddaughter.

The Butter Man

Authors: Elizabeth Alalou and Ali Alalou, Illustrator: Julie Klear Essakalli, Publisher: Charlesbridge, Year: 2008. **Social Studies Theme: Global Connections**

Too hungry to wait patiently for the couscous dinner to cook, Nora moans to her Baba that she's "staaarving!" Taking Nora on his knee, Baba shares the story of the butter man from his own childhood. After a season of drought and poor harvest, food became scarce in his home, and Ali's father left to look for work across the mountains. Soon bread was the only thing left to eat, and the piece his mother gave him each day was smaller and harder than the piece on the day before. To distract Ali from his hunger, his mother suggested that he go outside and wait for the butter man. Ali could ask for a bit of butter to spread on his bread. The butter man doesn't pass by on that day, or any of the following days, but Ali is occupied by watching the villagers on the road. Finally, one of the travelers on the road is his own father, returning from across the mountains and carrying vegetables and a piece of meat. An author's note and glossary provide additional information about life in the High Atlas Mountains of Morocco.

How I Learned Geography

Author: Uri Shulevitz, Publisher: Farrar, Straus, and Giroux, Year: 2005.
Social Studies Theme: Global Connections

In an autobiographical story, Shulevitz describes his early childhood in Turkestan. At a time when his family was very poor and hungry, his father spent what little money they had on a map of the world instead of on food. After getting over his initial anger and disappointment, young Uri developed a fascination with the map, at first for the bright colors, and then for the details that would spur his artistic imagination, as he dreamed of far-away places he could visit vicariously. An author's note at the end includes a photograph of the author at age seven, as well as two drawings he did while he was a child: a map of Africa, drawn when he was ten, and a marketplace in Turkestan, drawn when he was 13.

Biblioburro

Author: Jeanette Winter, Publisher: Beach Lane Books, Year: 2010.
Social Studies Theme: Global Connections

Luis loves books so much, he figures out a way to share his passion with people living in rural areas of Colombia. Loading books into crates he's built for the backs of two burros, Alfa and Beto, Luis creates a "Biblioburro"—The Burro Library. Every week Luis and his Biblioburro travel "across the countryside to faraway villages in the lonely hills." The trips are long, lonely, and sometimes dangerous, but once he arrives at his destination, Luis insists on reading aloud to the children, who gather before they choose books to borrow. An author's note tells of the real Luis Soriana, who has delivered books by burro to remote Colombian villages since 2000.

Goal!

Author: Mina Javaherbin, Illustrator: A. G. Ford, Publisher: Candlewick, Year: 2010.
Social Studies Theme: Global Connections

The Iranian author of a story set in South Africa writes in a note: "Football is magic to me. Where there is a ball, there is hope, laughter, and strength." And her story's young narrator has a wonderful ball—"a federation-sized football that he won for being the best reader in his class." No longer do he and his friends have to play with cheap plastic balls most kids own. They have everything they need for a great game of soccer, but when they play in the streets of their town, they have to draw straws to see who will be the roof guard, on the lookout for bullies who would steal the wonderful ball. A. G. Ford's realistic oil paintings give a strong sense of a hardscrabble, sun-baked town even as they illustrate the universal details of a game played by children around the world. And even though the streets are never safe for these children, there is always a game to be played. As the narrator says, "When we play, we forget to worry. When we run, we are not afraid."

Mirror

Author: Jeannie Baker, Publisher: Candlewick Press, Year: 2010.
Social Studies Theme: Global Connections

Two interconnected stories comprise this innovative picture book about two boys in different parts of the world. One lives in Australia and one lives in Morocco. An introduction in both English and Arabic precedes each wordless visual narrative. The story set in Australia unfolds in pages that turn from right to left, and the story set in Morocco unfolds in pages that turn from left to right in this ingeniously designed work, in which the two stories are meant to be read side-by-side. In each story, the boys are seen starting the day at home with their families and then accompanying their fathers on errands. For the boy in Morocco, this involves a trip by donkey to a market to sell the rug his mother has woven. For the boy in Australia, it's running around the city by car picking up various home improvement items, including a beautiful new carpet—the same one the Moroccan mother wove. The illustrations capture the crowded cityscape in Australia, the openness of the Moroccan landscape, and the abundance of choices found in both "Hardware Planet" and a Moroccan bazaar with equal skill.

Culture

Social studies programs should include experiences that provide for the study of culture and cultural diversity (http://www.socialstudies.org/standards/strands).

Cultures are dynamic and ever changing. The study of culture prepares students to ask and answer questions such as: What are the common characteristics of different cultures? How do belief systems, such as religion or political ideals of the culture, influence the other parts of the culture? How does the culture change to accommodate different ideas and beliefs? What does language tell us about the culture? In schools, this theme typically appears in units and courses dealing with geography, history, and anthropology, as well as multicultural topics across the curriculum.

In elementary education the exploration of the concepts of likeness and differences in subjects such as language arts, mathematics, science, music, and art makes the study of culture essential. The young learners are or will be interacting with other students, some of whom are alike and some different. Obviously students may want to know more about others.

- This theme deals with geography, history, and anthropology, language arts, mathematics, science, music, and art.
- Culture and cultural diversity.

Time, Change, and Continuity

Human beings seek to understand their historical roots and locate themselves in time (http://www.socialstudies.org/standards/strands).

Activities for Time, Change, and Continuity

- Discuss history and share books on historical fiction with students.
- Provide the context of historical events so that students have prior knowledge.
- Create awareness of family life in various places, now and in the past.
- Analyze clothes, homes, food, communication, and cultural traditions.

Global Connections

Social studies programs should include experiences that provide for the study of global connection and interdependence (http://www.socialstudies.org/standards/strands).

FURTHER TEXTS

The realities of global interdependence require understanding the increasingly important and diverse global connections among world communities. Analysis of tensions between national interests and global priorities contributes to the development of possible solutions to persistent and emerging global issues in many fields such as health care, economic development, environmental quality, universal human rights, etc. Analyzing patterns and relationships within and among world cultures such as economic competition and interdependence, age-old ethnic enmities, and political and military alliances help students examine policy alternatives that have both national and global implications. This theme appears in units and lessons dealing with geography, culture, and economics, natural and physical sickness, and humanities, including literature, the arts, and language. Through exposure to various media and first-hand experiences, young learners become aware of and are affected by events on a global scale. Within this context, elementary students examine and explore global connections and basic issues and concerns, suggesting and initiating responsive action plans.

This theme deals with geography, culture, economics, humanities, literature, and language arts (http://www.socialstudies.org/standards/strands).

Activities for Global Connections

- Develop an understanding of the increasingly diverse world communities.
- Analyze tensions between national interests and global priorities.
- Develop possible solutions to emerging global issues in many fields.
- Analyze patterns and relationships within and among world cultures.
- Examine policy alternatives that have both national and global implications.

This section defines and explains the selected thematic strands (Culture, Time, Continuity, and Change; Global Connections). The explanations give examples of questions that may be asked within each thematic strand as well as appropriate children's trade books. Furthermore, activities that bring the social studies standards and children's literature together are suggested.

References

Arora Lal, Sunandini. *Countries of the World: India*. Milwaukee: Gareth Stevens, 1999. An introduction to the geography, history, economy, culture, and people of the second-most populous country in the world.

Badt, Karin Luisa. *Greetings!* A World of Difference Series. Danbury, CT: Children's Press, 1994. Greetings from around the world are presented through text and illustrations. From handshakes to bows and hugs, greetings vary throughout the world.

Dooley, Norah and Thornton, Peter. *Everybody Cooks Rice*. New York: Scholastic, 1991. Carrie hunts for Anthony in almost everyone else's kitchen on the block, where they both discover that everybody cooks rice.

Ford, Juwanda and Wilson-Max, Ken. *K is for Kwanzaa: A Kwanzaa Alphabet Book*. New York: Scholastic, 1997. Celebrates the African-American holiday Kwanzaa by introducing related words from A to Z.

Ganeri, Anita and Wright, Rachel. *Mexico*. Country Topics for Craft Projects Series. New York: Franklin Watts, 1994. An introduction to Mexico, its history, and culture is combined with information about food, sports, festivals, and crafts.

Myers, Walter Dean and Myers, Christopher. *Harlem*. New York: Scholastic, 1997. Words and pictures connect readers of all ages to the spirit of Harlem in its music, art, literature, and everyday life, and to how it has helped shape us as a people.

Raczek, Linda Theresa and Bennett, Gary. *Rainy's Powwow*. Flagstaff, AZ: Rising Moon, 1999. This story celebrates a vanishing way of life that embodies the long-standing traditions of becoming welcomed into the powwow family. A glossary of powwow terms and dances is included.

Say, Allen. *Grandfather's Journey*. Boston: Houghton Mifflin, 1993. A Japanese-American recounts his grandfather's journey to America, which he later also undertakes, and the feelings of being torn by a love for two different countries.

Shea, Pegi Dietz and Riggio, Anita. *The Whispering Cloth*. New York: Boyds Mills, 1995. Mai, a Hmong girl living in Thailand, wants to tell her family experience by stitching a pa'ndau story cloth.

Viesti, Joe and Hall, Diane. *Celebrate! In Central America*. New York: Lothrop, Lee, and Shepard, 1998. The text begins with a map and introduction to the countries in Central America. Children will have a visual experience of many celebrations. Large, colorful pictures with limited text make celebrations come alive.

FURTHER TEXTS

Time, Continuity, and Change

Social studies programs should include experiences that provide for the study of the ways human beings view themselves in and over time (http://www.socialstudies.org/standards/strands).

Human beings seek to understand their historical roots and locate themselves in time. Such understanding involves knowing what things were like in the past and how things change and develop. Knowing how to read and reconstruct the past allows one to develop a historical perspective and to answer questions such as: Who am I? What happened in the past? How am I connected to those in the past? How has the world changed and how might it change in the future? This theme appears in courses in history.

K–5 learners gain experience with sequencing to establish a sense of order and time. They enjoy hearing stories of the recent past as well as of remote past. They also recognize that people may hold different views about the past and understand the relationship between human decisions and consequences. Discussing history and sharing books on historical fiction with students is rewarding because they learn about their own heritage, as well as other cultures.

When selecting trade books, teachers should ensure that characters' actions, language, style of living, and values are realistic for the time period. The setting needs to be authentic and the theme worthwhile. It is important to provide instruction about the content of historical events so that students have prior knowledge to help them make connection to the people, places, and events described in the book. Students should also be aware of family life in various places, now and in the past. They should be able to analyze clothes, homes, food, communication, and cultural traditions. This will help to lay the foundation for the development of historical knowledge, skills, and values.

FURTHER TEXTS

References

Macdonald, Fiona. *A Child's Eye View of History*. New York: Simon & Schuster, 1998. This book includes stories of real children from the past and describes some of the toys and games used in ancient times. For example, an Egyptian wooden toy lion more than 3,500 years old and a yo-yo from 400 B.C.

Carlson, Laurie. *More than Moccasins: A Kid's Activity Guide to Traditional North American Indian Life*. Chicago: Chicago review press, 1994. This book holds more than 100 illustrated crafts and activities that encourage students to have fun and be creative as they learn about Native American life and values.

Fritz, Jean, et al. *The World in 1492*. New York: Trumpet Club, 1992. Pictures, maps, and drawings complement text that tells what the world was like in 1492. The book includes chapters on Europe, Asia, Africa, Australia, Oceania, and the Americas.

Moore, Kay and O'Leary, Daniel. *If You Lived at the Time of the American Revolution*. New York: Scholastic, 1997. This book tells about Americans' fight to be free and independent. It tells what it was like to be a Patriot who supported the war or a Loyalist who did not want to break away from England.

Schanzer, Rosalyn. *How We Crossed the West: The Adventures of Lewis and Clark*. Washington, DC: National Geographic Society, 1997. The 1804 expedition of Meriwether Lewis and William Clark is shared. Quotes from the explorers' journals and large, colorful pictures help the reader to experience their exploits and discoveries.

Polacco, Patricia. *Pink and Say*. New York: Scholastic, 1994. The dangers of war are shared in a touching story as told by two young soldiers during the civil war.

Ross, Alice; Ross, Kent; and Bowman, Leslie. *The Copper Lady*. Minneapolis: Carolrhoda books, 1997. After helping Monsieur Bartholdi to build the statue of liberty, a Parisian orphan stows away on the ship carrying the statue to America.

Fritz, Jean and DiSalvo-Ryan, DyAnne. *You Want Women to Vote, Lizzie Stanton?* New York: G.P. Putnam's Sons, 1995. The story's narrator is Elizabeth Cady Stanton, who did not live to see women get the vote but who is strongly associated with the fight for women's suffrage.

Houston, Gloria and Cooney, Barbara. *The Year of the Perfect Christmas Tree*. New York: Dial, 1988. The book tells the story of an Appalachian Christmas during World War I and a special family responsibility because the father is off to war.

Lied, Kate; Lied, Ernst; and Campbell, Lisa. *Potato: A Tale from the Great Depression*. Washington, DC: National Geographic Society, 1997. During the Great Depression, a family seeking work finds two weeks of employment digging potatoes in Idaho.

Roy, Deborah Kogan. *My Daddy Was a Soldier: A World War II Story*. New York: Holiday House, 1990. While her father is fighting in the Pacific, Jeannie plants a victory garden, collects scrap, and sends letters to her father as she anxiously awaits his return.

Kustanowitz, Esther. *The Hidden Children of the Holocaust: Teens Who Hid from the Nazis*. New York: Rosen, 1999. In their own words, Jewish teenagers tell of their experiences hiding from the Nazis. A timeline, glossary, bibliography, photos, and website addresses are included in this 64-page book.

Smith, Carter. *The Korean War*. Englewood Cliffs, NJ: Silver Burdett, 1990. This book describes the people, places, and events surrounding the Korean War, using original source photos, maps, and artwork.

Wright, David. *A Multicultural Portrait of the Vietnam War*. Tarrytown, NY: Benchmark Books, 1996. The Vietnam War is discussed from a multicultural point of view. Photos, maps, a timeline, a glossary, and suggestions for further reading all add to the text of the book.

FURTHER TEXTS

Foster, Leila Merrell. *The Story of the Persian Gulf War.* Danbury, CT: Children's Press, 1991. This book examines the causes and events of the Persian Gulf War that followed Iraq's invasion of Kuwait in 1990. It explains how the United States got involved in Operation Desert Shield and then Operation Desert Storm.

Global Connections

Social studies programs should include experiences that provide for the study of global connection and interdependence (http://www.socialstudies.org/standards/strands).

The realities of global interdependence require understanding the increasingly important and diverse global connections among world communities. Analysis of tensions between national interests and global priorities contributes to the development of possible solutions to persistent and emerging global issues in many fields such as health care, economic development, environmental quality, universal human rights, etc. Analyzing patterns and relationships within and among world cultures such as economic competition and interdependence, age-old ethnic enmities, and political and military alliances helps students examine policy alternatives that have both national and global implications. This theme appears in units and lessons dealing with geography, culture, and economics, natural and physical sickness, and humanities, including literature, the arts, and language. Through exposure to various media and first-hand experiences, young learners become aware of and are affected by events on a global scale. Within this context, elementary students examine and explore global connections and basic issues and concerns, suggesting and initiating responsive action plans.

FURTHER TEXTS

Selecting Children's Picture Books to Teach Social Studies Themes

NCSS Standards	Picture Books	Suggested Activities
1. Culture	Arora Lal, Sunandini. (1999). *Countries of the World: India*. Milwaukee: Gareth Stevens. An introduction to the geography, history, economy, culture, and people. David Wisniewski. (1992). *Sundiata: Lion King of Mali*. Clarion Books. Inspiring story of courage, determination, and bravery in the time when Africa had empires, kings, and emperors. The story is supplemented with pictures.	Help children understand another culture by creating a culture box. Learn about children from another country. Focus on the similarities of culture. Invite a guest speaker to tell the story and ask students to find historical characters in other cultures with similar courage and determination like Sundiata.
2. Time, continuity, change	Fritz, Jean, et al. (1992). *The World in 1492*. New York: Trumpet Club. Pictures, maps, and drawings complement text that tells what the world was like in 1492. The book includes chapters on Europe, Asia, Africa, Australia, Oceania, and the Americas. Schanzer, Rosalyn. (1997). *How We Crossed the West: The Adventures of Lewis and Clark*. Washington, DC: National Geographic Society. The 1804 expedition of Meriwether Lewis and William Clark is shared in an adventurous manner. Polacco, Patricia. (1994) Pink and Say. New York: Scholastic. The dangers of war are shared in a touching story as told by two young soldiers during the civil war.	After reading the book, *You Want Women to Vote, Lizzie Stanton?*, students write and act out short plays from each segment of women's history, ranging from no rights in the early 1800s to the passage of the Nineteenth Amendment in 1920 to the push for an equal rights amendment and the current call for equity in the job market. For historical understanding, ask students to write their own historical narratives. Ask students to follow the expedition of Lewis and Clark on a map. Younger learners can draw a picture of their favorite travel experience from the book. Older students could write a reaction to what life would be like if they were on the trip with the explorers.

3. People, places, environment	Ancona, George. (1982). *Bananas. From Manolo to Marge.* Clarion Books. Highlights the patterns and networks of economic interdependence. Baker, Lucy. (1992). *Life in the Deserts: Animals, People, Plants.* New York: Scholastic. The location of major deserts is shown on a map. Cherry, Lynne. (1992). *A River Ran Wild.* New York: Trumpet. This is an environmental history of a river from early human settlement to the building of manufacturing plants that pollute the river. Dineen, Jacqueline. (1993). *Natural Disasters: Hurricanes and Typhoons.* New York: Shooting Star Press. Factual information about the formation and monitoring of, and the destruction caused by hurricanes is presented with pictures of actual storms.	Read the book, natural disasters. Make a KWL chart (what I KNOW; What I want to learn, what I Learned). Discuss these storms' effects on the earth's surface and on humans. *Geography for Life* suggests: List ways in which people adapt to the physical environment (example: choices of clothing, housing styles, agricultural practices, recreational activities, food). Compare Cinderella stories from different geographic locations. How does the geography of the area change the tone of the story? Describe the geography of the region, find the countries on a world map, and locate illustrations of natural vegetation.
4. Identity	Hamanaka, Sheila. (1994). *All the Colors of the World.* Mulberry Books. Despite physical differences all children are the same. Birdseye, Debbie and Birdseye, Tome. (1997). *Under Our Skin: Kids Talk About Race.* New York: Holiday House. Six students talk about their ethnic backgrounds and experiences with people of different races.	Students from other races find out about other children's favorite foods, games, songs, dreams, likes, and dislikes. Students list the similarities in categories. Read the stories and have students share their experiences related to the book.

FURTHER TEXTS

5. Individual, groups, institutions	Benjamin, Anne and Beier, Ellen. (1996). *Young Rosa Parks: Civil Rights Heroine.* Mahwah, NJ: Troll Associates.	Ask students to name their favorite famous person, whether dead or alive, and discuss why he/she is their favorite.
	Fisher, Leonard Everett. (1995). *Ghandi.* New York: Atheneum. The Life of Mohandas Karamchand Gandhi (1869–1948). He is famous for fighting for racial equality and civil rights.	Ask students to write about what they liked about Gandhi, Benjamin Franklin, Martin Luther King Jr., and Rosa Parks. Challenge students to think about their own role in institutional change.
6. Power, authority, governance		Create a bulletin board titled "Our Government at Work"; have students list different bodies of the government; get them to form groups; and have each group belong to a body. Discuss their roles at the local/state/federal level. Discuss how decisions made by each body affect them personally.
7. Production, distribution, consumption	Carle, Eric. (1990). *Pancakes, Pancakes!* New York: Scholastic. Jack wants a pancake for lunch; he needs flour from the miller, eggs from hens, and milk from cows.	Select different books on food to read. Students discuss resources, food production, wants, and needs. Read the school lunch menu and discuss the economic process needed to have various items on the menu.

FURTHER TEXTS

8. Science, technology, society	Freedman, Russell. (1991). *The Wright Brothers: How They Invented the Airplane*. New York: Scholastic. The book traces the lives of Wilbur and Orville Wright and their contributions to society.	Ask students to make a chart of advances in transportation, communication, health and nutrition and their impact on their daily lives and the society.
	Hudson, Wade and Garnett, Ron. (1995). *Great Black Heroes: Five Notable Inventors*. New York: Scholastic.	List contributions of inventors from other races; discussion on the notion that "Science has no boundaries."
	Stille, Darlene. *Extraordinary Women Scientists*. Danbury, CT: Children's Press.	

FURTHER TEXTS

9. Global connections	Fox, Mem and Wilton, Nicholas. (1996). *Feathers and Fools.* New York: Harcourt Brace. Modern fable about peacocks and swans who allow the fear of their differences to destroy them.	Discuss the importance of getting along with others so that conflicts do not occur. Look at the books *Why* and *Feathers and Fools* to help students understand how conflicts can escalate.
	Javna, John. (1990). *50 Simple Things Kids Can Do to Save the Earth.* New York: Scholastic. Includes a variety of interesting and purposeful activities that children can do to make a difference in saving the environment.	In cooperative teams, have each team select one activity or game from the book and work on the project. Share the completed projects with the entire classroom.
	Milord, Susan. (1999). *Hands Around the World: 365 Creative Ways to Build Cultural Awareness and Global Respect.* Milwaukee: Gareth Stevens. Includes a variety of games and other activities to promote awareness of different cultures.	After reading sections to the students from *A World in Our Hands,* provide each student with paper to write or draw what they would like the world to know about such topics as struggle for peace or children's rights. Put these together in a classroom book.
		Saving the environment is a global concern. Show students that they can make a difference in protecting the environment for the benefit of all people. In cooperative groups, select one suggestion from the book, *50 Simple Things Kids Can Do to Save the Earth*.
		In cooperative teams, have each team select one activity or game from the book and work on the project. Share the completed projects with the entire classroom.

10. Civic engagement	Fritz, Jean. (1993). *Just a Few Words, Mr. Lincoln: The Story of the Gettysburg Address*. New York: Scholastic. The story of President Lincoln delivering his 271-word speech, recounted with pictures.	
	King, Martin Luther, Jr. (1997). *I Have a Dream*. New York: Scholastic.	
	Stein, R. Conrad (1995). *The Declaration of Independence*. Danbury, CT: Children's Press.	

Group Activity # 1

Select five books from the picture book column to match with five standards in the NCSS standards column. Discuss the rationale for your choice and justify the matching. Suggest activities that students will be able to do in the activities column.

NCSS Standards	High-Quality Picture Books	Activities
1. People, places, environment		
2. Individual, groups, institutions		
3. Production, distribution, consumption		

Group Activity # 2

Select and list five books in the picture book column to match with five standards in the NCSS standards column. Discuss the rationale for your choice and justify the matching. Suggest activities that students will be able to do in the activities column.

NCSS Standards	Picture Books	Activities
1. Culture		
2. Time, continuity, change		
3. People, places, environment		
4. Identity		
5. Individual, groups, institutions		
6. Power, authority, governance		
7. Production, distribution, consumption		

FURTHER TEXTS

8. Science, technology, society		
9. Global connections		
10. Civic engagement		

References

Butchart, Ronald E. and Barbara McEwan. (1998). *Classroom Discipline in American Schools: Problems and Possibilities for Democratic Education*. New York: New York Press.

Cangelosi, J.S. (2000). *Classroom Management Strategies: Gaining and Maintaining Students' Cooperation*. New York: John Wiley & Sons.

Charles, C.M. (2002). *Building Classroom Discipline*. Boston: Allyn and Bacon.

Charles, C.M. and Senter, W.G. (2002). *Elementary Classroom Management*. Boston: Allyn and Bacon.

Dinkelman, T. (2003). "Self-Study in Teacher Education: A Means and Ends Tool for Promoting Reflective Teaching." *Journal of Teacher Education*, 54 6–18.

Eby, J.W. (1997). *Reflective Planning, Teaching, and Evaluation for the Elementary School*. Upper Saddle River, NJ: Merrill, Prentice Hall.

Gartrell, D. (2003). *A Guidance Approach for the Encouraging Classroom*. Canada: Delmar Learning.

Geiger, B. (2000). "Discipline in K Through 8th Grade Classrooms." *Education*, 121, 383.

Henderson, G.J. (1992). *Reflective Teaching: Becoming an Inquiring Educator*. New York: Macmillan.

Jarolimek, J. (1990). *Social Studies in Elementary Education*. New York: Macmillan.

FURTHER TEXTS

Jean Pierre, B. (2004). "Two Urban Elementary Science Classrooms: The Interplay Between Student Interactions and Classroom Management Practices." *Education*, 124, 664–678.

Kauffman, J.M., Mostert, M.P., Trent, C.S., and Hallahan, D.P. (2002). *Managing Classroom Behavior: A Reflective Case-Based Approach*. Boston.: Allyn and Bacon.

Kounin, J. (1977). *Discipline and Group Management in Classrooms*. New York: Holt, Rinehart and Winston.

Loughran, J.J. (2002). "Effective Reflective Practice: In Search of Meaning in Learning About Teaching." *Journal of Teacher Education*, Jan–Feb 2002.

Manke, M.P. (1997). *Classroom Power Relations: Understanding Student-Teacher Interaction*. Mahwah, NJ: Lawrence Erlbaum.

Marzano, J.R. (2003). *What Works in Schools: Translating Research into Action*. Alexandria, VA: Association for Supervision and Curriculum Development.

Rimm-Kaufman, S., La Paro, K., Downer, J., and Pianta R.C. (2005). "The Contribution of Classroom Setting and Quality of Instruction to Children's Behavior in Kindergarten Classrooms." *The Elementary School Journal*, March 2005 v105, 377–395.

Ross, D.L. (2002). "Cooperating Teachers Facilitating Reflective Practice for Student Teachers in a Professional Development School." *Education*, Summer, 7–12.

Traynor, P.L (2002). "A Scientific Evaluation of Five Strategies Teachers Use to Maintain Order." *Education*, 122, 493–511.

Traynor, P.L. (2003). "Factors Contributing to Teacher Choice of Classroom Order Strategies." *Education*, 123, 586 (14).

Maxim, G.W.(2003). *Social Studies and the Elementary School Child*. Upper Saddle River, NJ: Merrill.

Welton, D.A. (2002). *Children and Their World*. (7th ed.). Boston: Houghton Mifflin.

FURTHER TEXTS

CLASS ASSIGNMENTS

Class Assignment and Sample Research Projects

Suggested Assignment Protocols

For this assignment you will use some class time or outside the class time in order to achieve excellence. You must not use this time to work on assignments from other classes. You are expected to meet the deadlines in this class.

You must submit an abstract as soon as you identify your research topic. I will be working with you all the way as a coach making suggestions for improvement before presenting.

Option A: Research

Step one: Identify an issue, problem, or topic to be researched from a social studies textbook, the core democratic values, social studies themes, or current events

- As a team, discuss and write an abstract (see example). (50 pts)

Step two: Team Planning

- Develop a list of questions that could serve as the focus of your investigation.
- Discuss and write a plan describing how you will carry out the research.
- Visit with your professor with your research/inquiry outline. (50 pts)

Step three: Carry out the investigation

- Gather and analyze findings/data.
- Write a summary of your findings.
- Use illustrations, quotes, photographs, charts, or graphs to share numeric data. (150 pts)

Step four: Present your findings and conclusions

- Each team report should last 15 – 20 minutes. (150 pts)

Step five: Individual Reflection. (100 pts)

1. What knowledge, skills, and dispositions have you mastered as a result of **doing** this assignment? (20 pts)
2. Give at least three specific ways in which this assignment has prepared you for your future social studies classroom. (20 pts)
3. Based on your experience doing the assignment, what you do you now know to be the purpose of social studies education? As far as the discussions in class, do you think it is essential

to engage your future students in research or historical inquiry projects? Give at least three reasons. (30 pts)

4. Keep a detailed record of the total time spent on the inquiry from the start to the completion. (30 pts)

OR

Option B: Historical Inquiry

In social studies, terms such as problem solving, reflective thinking (Dewey), and discovery learning (Bruner) are used to describe inquiry-based activities.

The National Standards for History expect students in elementary school to think and act like historians.

Step one: Identify the historical issue, problem, event, or current topic to be investigated

- Write an abstract.
- Choose the method of investigation (interview, primary sources, document analysis, trip to museums, and observation).
- Develop a list of questions that could serve as the focus of your inquiry. (50 pts)

Step two: Plan the inquiry

- Decide what resources you will need.
- Write an outline describing how you will carry out the inquiry.
- Visit with your professor and have your inquiry outline with you. (50 pts)

Step three: Carry out the inquiry

- Analyze and write a summary of your findings.
- Use illustrations, quotes, photographs, artifacts, etc. (150 pts)

Step four: Present what you learned as a result of your inquiry

- In-class report should last 15 – 20 minutes.

Step five: Individual reflection. (100 pts)

1. What knowledge, skills, and dispositions have you mastered as a result of doing this assignment? 20 pts.
2. Give at least three specific ways in which this assignment has prepared you for your future social studies classroom. 20 pts.

3. Based on your experience doing the assignment, what do you now know to be the purpose of social studies education? As far as the discussions in class, do you think it is essential to engage your future students in research or historical inquiry projects? Give at least three reasons. (30 pts) (You will lose one point for each typo, spelling, or grammar error.)
4. Keep a detailed record of the total time spent on the inquiry from the start to the completion. (30 pts)
5. Hand in your reflection before giving your presentation. You will earn an individual grade. (You will lose one point for each typo, spelling, or grammar error.)

Identifying the Issue, Problem, or Topic.

1. As a group, examine the causes and effects of the issue and then brainstorm potential projects to address the needs identified.

Researching the Issue

2. The first step in narrowing your focus is to learn more about the issue or issues you identified; you need to read the literature to find some factual information about the issue in your community.
3. When you begin to plan a service-learning project, it is important to involve the community from the very beginning. What are the social issues that the community is facing? What are the needs of local schools, parks, or other?

You may already have a passion for a particular issue, such as education, the environment, the economy, or disaster preparedness/response. However, a community-needs assessment is still an important part of designing any service project. Assessing community needs can be as simple as taking a walk through your neighborhood or as complex as surveying the entire school. By working together with K–12 community members, you will build their awareness and help ensure some buy-in and support for your service efforts. You can use a variety of methods to assess community needs. You should select one that fits the scope of your students' interest and academic needs. For a one-day project, you may want to choose an assessment technique that is less time-consuming.

Here are some ideas for conducting a community-needs assessment:

Deciding on a Project

Once you have assessed the needs of the community and researched the issue, it is important to define your scope.

When selecting a project, pay close attention to:

- Required time or days to complete the project.
- Overall project scope: Can the project be scaled up or down as needed?

- Ongoing projects engage students on a consistent basis, providing the opportunity to go beyond a one-time experience and have a sustained experience and impact in the community.

Reflection

Reflection is an important part of a service-learning project. Reflection is a process through which students think about their personal experiences.

Throughout the project, provide time for students to think and talk about their service experience. As students engage in reflection, they develop a sense of accomplishment, establish a deeper connection to the benefactors of their service, and deepen their understanding of the social issue they dealt with. Reflection is designed to encourage students to examine the project in terms of what they did, what they learned, how it affected them, and how they will continue to support the social issue.

Students can have a group discussion, write about their experience, create a photo journal and captions of the project, or respond to quotes about service. When planning your project, decide which form of reflection you want students to use. Tailor the reflection activity to the project.

For example, if students are assisting with arts and crafts classes at a daycare center, they can create a simple art project about their service experience.

Examples of Students' Research Projects and Reflection

Research Project #1: Diversity: How K–12 Schools Accommodate Learners From Diverse Backgrounds

Alyssa Zizio and Ashley Cleary

ABSTRACT

This research focuses or the effect diversity has on the culture in K–12 schools and how students of different backgrounds are accommodated. Research and studies illustrate information on how the United States public school systems have done a poor job educating different backgrounds of children, such as Hispanics, African Americans, children of poverty and immigration students (2007). Statistics show the achievement gaps between Black, White, and Hispanic children in the classroom (2009). Our hypothesis is that K–12 schools are not providing enough accommodations to students that are from diverse backgrounds. Our goal is to gain insight as prospective teachers on how diversity is promoted and enhanced in K–12 schools. We will assess the effect diversity has in the classroom in Maple, Oak, Waterford and Willow* Public School Systems. We will be interview-

---

* Names have been changed.

CLASS ASSIGNMENTS

ing at least one teacher at each school to find out about culturally diverse children and how they are accommodated in the classroom.

ACHIEVEMENT GAP

According to GreatSchools.org, "Many diverse schools experience an achievement gap, meaning that some groups of students achieve at a much higher level than other groups, especially on standardized tests. It is common to see persistent patterns of underachievement for lower-income, African American, and Hispanic students on standardized test scores."

Percentages of Proficiency in State Schools For Writing

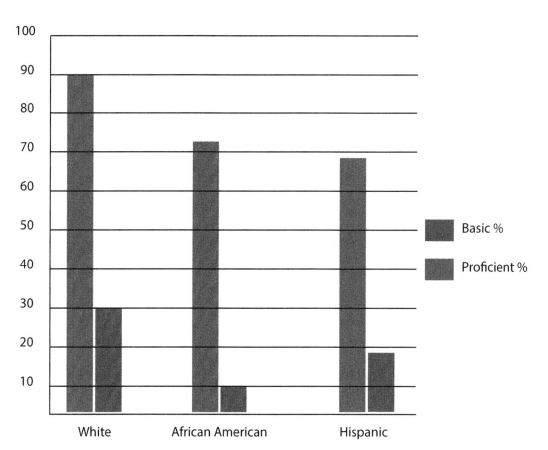

2011 State Average Percentages of Student Proficiency in 8th Grade Reading

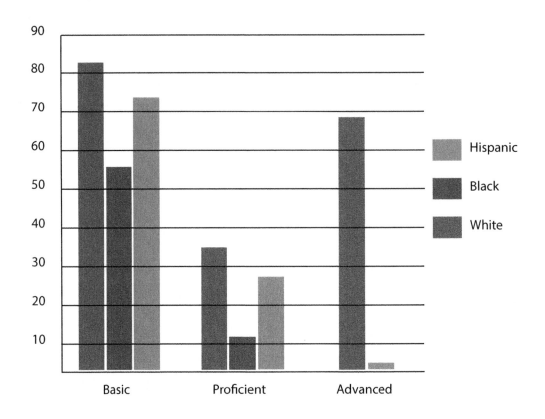

CLASS ASSIGNMENTS

INTERVIEW QUESTIONS

1. How many students are in your classroom this year?
2. How many students in your classroom come from different backgrounds that are non-white?
3. Do the children of different backgrounds in your classroom frequently disrupt the learning environment?
4. Do you notice an overall difference in academic performance in the language arts content area (reading and writing) between non-white and white students?
5. What are some things you would suggest to other teachers to help accommodate students that are struggling in school?

INTERVIEWS: MS. C
GRADE 4 – MAPLE ELEMENTARY SCHOOL

1. How many students are in your classroom this year?
   28

2. How many students in your classroom come from different backgrounds that are non-white?
   0

3. Do the children of different backgrounds in your classroom frequently disrupt the learning environment?
   Maple is not very diverse. Special needs children can be more of a disruption, if we are not able to meet their needs.

4. Do you notice an overall difference in academic performance in the language arts content area (reading and writing) between non-white and white students?
   Maple is not very diverse, so this is not true.

5. What are some things you would suggest to other teachers to help accommodate students that are struggling in school?
   Be patient and take the time to work with students and parents. Make what's going on in school easy for the parents to know and understand. Remember that most parents are doing the best they can in their situation.

INTERVIEWS: MS. L
GRADE 4 – MAPLE ELEMENTARY SCHOOL

1. How many students are in your classroom this year?
   29

2. How many students in your classroom come from different backgrounds that are non-white?
   1

3. Do the children of different backgrounds in your classroom frequently disrupt the learning environment?
   Absolutely not. We have very few students that are ethnically different and those that we do have just blend in with the other students.

4. Do you notice an overall difference in academic performance in the language arts content area (reading and writing) between non-white and white students?
   Normally I would say no but this year my non-white student is from Thailand and is an ESL student, so yes she struggles with comprehension but her decoding and fluency are at grade level.

5. What are some things you would suggest to other teachers to help accommodate students that are struggling in school?
   I try to get to know my students and their families. Understanding their outlook on the importance of school helps to understand why some students do well and others do not.

INTERVIEWS: MS. C
GRADES 9–11 – WILLOW HIGH SCHOOL

1. How many students are in your classroom?
1st hour, Honors Geometry: 29; 2nd/3rd hours, Algebra II, double block: 13; 5th hour, Honors Geometry: 16; 6th hour, Honors Geometry: 18.

2. How many students in you classroom come from different backgrounds that are non-white?
Honors Geometry: 5 kids total; Algebra II with double block: 11 total

3. Do the children of different backgrounds in your classroom frequently disrupt the learning environment?
Not in the honors classes, but I couldn't say just the students with different backgrounds disrupt the learning environment in my Algebra II with double block. My Algebra ll class is for the very low struggling learner. The class is two periods long instead of just one, so the students are together longer. Disruptions are daily. A lot of these students don't have great home lives and have bigger issues than behaving. On average, my students who are from different backgrounds do disrupt the classroom environment more than the white students, but that is not to say that all of them do.

4. Do you notice an overall difference in academic performance in the language arts content (reading and writing) between non-white and white students?
For the most part, the students who have a lot of trouble reading and writing are minority students—specifically African American—at [Willow].

5. What are some things you would suggest to other teachers to help accommodate students that are struggling in school?
I would want to say that a lot of the time, it seems like students struggle in school for different reasons, and I think it is the teacher's job to understand his/her students and the reasons behind a student's behavior. Some teachers automatically think that students who don't do their homework, don't pay attention in class, or do poorly on tests/quizzes are just lazy students. Realistically, these students could have so much going on outside of school that they can't even concentrate or put any kind of time or energy into homework or studying. For example, for a student who has a missing parent figure (works 2nd or 3rd shifts), the student might be completely in charge of his/her sisters and brothers for the entire night and that student could be the "parent figure" for the younger siblings. A teacher might give adjusted assignments to that student, understanding he or she does not have the same amount of time in the evenings as other students.

INTERVIEWS: MS. H
GRADES 9–12—WILLOW HIGH SCHOOL

1. How many students are in your classroom this year?
   I have 148 students.

2. How many students in your classroom come from different backgrounds that are non-white?
   Forty-four of my students are from diverse backgrounds.

3. Do the children of different backgrounds in your classroom frequently disrupt the learning environment?
   No—disrupt is too strong a word. They do present a challenge because they are verbally outspoken.

4. Do you notice an overall difference in academic performance in the language arts content area (reading and writing) between non-white and white students?
   It is difficult to say simply for the fact that many of my diverse students do not turn the assignment in or attempt the exercise/class work. I cannot accurately say that my non-white students' academic performance is lower than my white students', but their follow-through on deadlines and their motivation to complete tasks certainly seems less.

5. What are some things you would suggest to other teachers to help accommodate students that are struggling in school?
   I see a disconnect between the curriculum and my population. The English department could certainly add more diverse text, which might encourage more student interest in school. In addition, the school could provide more outside tutoring programs before or after school as a way to maximize the time struggling learners are surrounded by academic content. Latchkey is an elementary school concept, but I feel that it could serve to be relevant at the high school level. I also feel that academic performance should be linked to privileges such as playing a sport or joining a club. Many of my student athletes do not perform well within the classroom, yet they are allowed to play. There must be consequences and rewards for good behavior.

INTERVIEWS: MR. B
ASPEN HIGH SCHOOL

1. How many students are in your classroom this year?
   AP is at 25.

2. How many students in your classroom come from different backgrounds that are non-white?
   On average 5–8 students per class are non-white.

3. Do the children of different backgrounds in your classroom frequently disrupt the learning environment?
   No, there is no correlation between ethnic background and behavior problems.

4. Do you notice an overall difference in academic performance in the language arts content area (reading and writing) between non-white and white students?
Again, student performance is not significantly correlated with ethnicity.

5. What are some things you would suggest to other teachers to help accommodate students that are struggling in school?
One, make full use of any reading specialists and special education professionals in your building, Two, maintain good relations with the psychologists/social workers/counselors in the building. Three, work with the parents of students to help them understand what is happening in your classroom and why it is important. Give parents insights into how they can help their children succeed in your class.

INTERVIEWS: MR. C
ASPEN MIDDLE SCHOOL
GRADE 8

1. How many students are in your classroom this year?
I have four LA classes with 29–31 students per class. I teach an intervention class, Guided Study, which has 5–8 students and an SRT, which has 22.

2. How many students in your classroom come from different backgrounds that are non-white?
Of my 118 student, 24 of them are non-white.

3. Do the children of different backgrounds in your classroom frequently disrupt the learning environment?
I don't believe so, no more than others. Percentage is about the same.

4. Do you notice an overall difference in academic performance in the language arts content area (reading and writing) between non-white and white students?
It is similar.

5. What are some things you would suggest to other teachers to help accommodate students that are struggling in school?
Students have to buy into their education; we have to make them understand that it's important. It is a difficult chore without parental support.

INTERVIEWS: MR. P
OAK MIDDLE SCHOOL
GRADE 8

1. How many students are in your classroom this year?
I have 111 students all together.

2. How many students in your classroom come from different backgrounds that are non-white?
   Twenty-three out of the 111 are from different backgrounds. This is 1/5 of the class.

3. Do the children of different backgrounds in your classroom frequently disrupt the learning environment?
   No, I did not notice a difference between the students.

4. Do you notice an overall difference in academic performance in the language arts content area (reading and writing) between non-white and white students?
   There is not really a general rule with this. Only Native Americans seemed to struggle as a group. This is not really a predictable thing.

5. What are some things you would suggest to other teachers to help accommodate students that are struggling in school?
   Make sure to give extra help to students after school and lunch. Make yourself available as much as possible to the students.

2010–2011 Average Percentages of Student Proficiency in Willow Public Schools: High School Reading/Writing

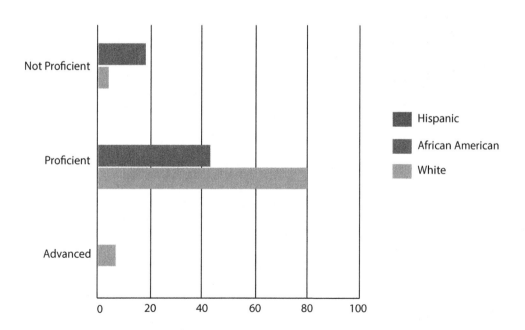

Willow High School Student Population

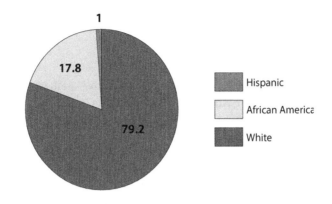

Maple School District

SUMMARY OF OUR FINDINGS

Percentages of Student Enrollment
2007

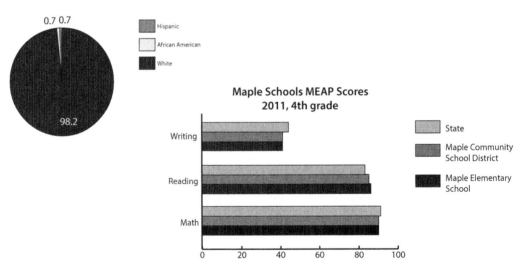

After gathering data showing the average scores for the reading and writing subject areas and comparing the basic and proficient scores between different races for the state, we noticed there was a large achievement gap between the different races. For the reading subject area, white students had 82% at the basic level, and 36% were at the proficient level. African American students had 54% basic and 11% proficient, and Hispanic students had 75% basic and 26% were at the proficient level (NCES). Based on this data, there is a clear achievement gap between the races in the reading subject area. For the writing subject area, the statistics are similar. At the basic level, there were 30% of white students, 73% African American students, and 68% Hispanic students. At the proficient level, there were 30% of white students, 10% of African American students, and 17% Hispanic students. When comparing this data as well, we can see the achievement gap. According to the NCES 2007 writing scores and the 2011 reading scores from where we got these statistics, the achievement gap between these races did not drastically change since 2002, so we wanted to see how to accommodate students of different races in order to help lessen the gap.

We interviewed teachers from the Oak, Maple, Aspen, and Willow school districts from the state. The Oak and Maple districts are non-urban environments. They had a less diverse student population than more urban schools. The few diverse students they do have in these schools usually just blend in with the other students and do not demonstrate more struggles in school than the white students. The Aspen and Willow school districts are urban areas and had more diversity in the schools. Some teachers from the Willow Schools did see an achievement gap between white and non-white students. A lot of the time, family and home life and environment can affect a student's learning and achievement in school. This is the case for some of the students who attend Willow High School. Although Willow and Aspen school districts are both urban areas, the overall achievement gap between the diverse races of the students differs. We were surprised by these results.

Oak Schools

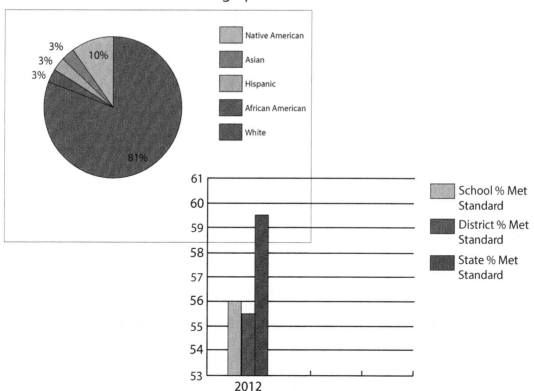

Oak Schools Student Demographics

CLASS ASSIGNMENTS

Aspen Public Schools

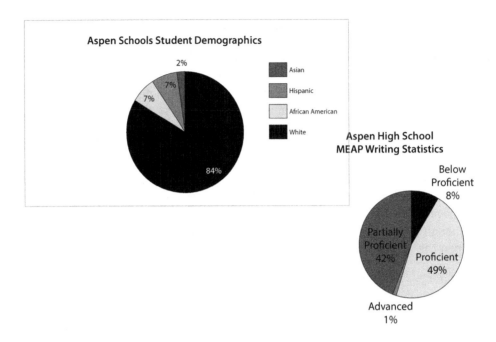

According to the teachers we interviewed, two out of the four schools did not notice an achievement gap in their classrooms when comparing white and non-white students. The overall statistics of the state illustrate that in the reading and writing content areas, there is an achievement gap between white and non-white students. We came to the conclusion that the race of a student is not the sole reason for an achievement gap between white, African American and Hispanic students. Students' performance in school can be influenced based on the area of the school, the environment in which they reside, and the educators.

A common theme that a majority of the teachers we interviewed suggested is that teachers need to get to know their students on a personal level. This includes checking out their family and personal life in order to understand why they are struggling in school. A lack of diverse literature and material can also affect a student's outlook of school and overall academic performance.

According to Ms. H., English teacher at Willow High School, "The English department could certainly add more diverse text, which might encourage more student interest in school." Students are interested in material that is relevant to their lives, so it is important for teachers to implement different types of literature and material into their classroom that will help students understand the different backgrounds and ethnicities that exist in the United States.

Accommodations should be made on an individualized basis. No matter race or ethnicity, it is important to make sure the students' parents and family are involved in their children's schooling. If the students' family does not care about their schooling then the students will have negative attitudes towards it as well.

REFLECTION ON OUR FINDINGS

The topic that we have been researching the past few weeks is the gender gap in the elementary-education profession. We were curious as to why there are fewer men in the elementary-education profession. Our group used a survey to find results on our topic. Each of us sent out our survey to multiple teachers whom we know. Most of us were given some sort of response. We were able to obtain comments for our survey from nine different teachers, most of whom, however, are female. One male teacher responded to the survey and even supplied us with a paper he wrote for one of his education classes. His paper dealt with the same topic we were conducting our research on. In our findings we are seeing a trend of low numbers of male elementary teachers in our schools. The research we have conducted gave results proving this to be true. What we are trying to find is why there are fewer males than females in our elementary teaching profession.

We asked the question: Have you noticed a gender gap within your school district? The answer that we were given was, "yes." One hundred percent of people who took our survey agreed that there is a gender gap in the school system they work in. This was across five different schools and districts. Our next question asked: What are the main reasons for the gender gap in the education profession? The majority of the responses were that men are more likely to work with older children because men are less nurturing than their female counterparts; they usually do not like working with young children. This is the stereotype portrayed by many men that they are not caring or nurturing enough to work with small children. Many people answered that males do not look upon the elementary-education profession with interest because it is not a high-paying career or manly. We also asked if the gender gap could be reduced and 88% of our participants said that it could. They gave us reasons as to how. The main answers were that academic counselors should bring about discussion for teaching in elementary grades to males who are seeking education in the teaching profession. Many participants had the same ideas where certain districts should try to hire more male elementary teachers. We also researched and asked the teachers if they believed that students should have more male role models in the elementary-education profession. Eighty-eight percent of the teacher participants agreed that students, especially boys, need more male role models in the elementary-education profession. Some even said that female students need more male teachers as role models. The only male to take our survey said that he has parents who request him because they feel as though he could impact their male students. Boys like having male teachers because they can relate to them. We then asked for stereotypes that our participants think help deter males from becoming teachers. The majority wrote that males are not compassionate enough, caring or nurturing enough, and that it is a low-paying profession. These are the main reasons we see fewer males. Another piece of information that we looked for was if there is a difference between the genders and their teaching. All agreed that there is no difference between the genders (one gender does not teach better than the other), but there is a difference between the teaching styles that each person, male or female, uses. Our next question dealt with whether or not male teachers receive different treatment among staff and coworkers. Eighty-eight percent of our participants said, "yes." Many said that male teachers are not given as many limitations or expectations. A few of our participants said that male teachers can get away with a lot; for example, not having to write lesson plans or not having to submit as many reports. They did say, however, that males receive more teasing from coworkers. This is especially true if the male is the minority. Many females believe that they are able to tease men because males use more humor in the classroom. When we asked if males were treated differently in a teaching program, many of the participants said that males were treated differently. The main answer was that males are pushed harder to complete elementary-education courses because there are so few of them in those courses. Multiple responses were the opposite, however, and they thought that the treatment was the same. Our final question we wanted answers to was: How many males are in your school? Forty-four percent said that it was zero to three, another 44% said four to eight, and the last 11% said that it was nine or more. This confirmed our results that the majority of schools have significantly lower numbers of male teachers than female teachers.

The male teacher who took our survey sent us a copy of one of his papers dealing with the gender gap in elementary education. His paper covers all of the topics that we set out to find research about. Many of the topics he discussed were the stereotypes that deter male educators from the elementary profession. They are that men are not caring, nurturing, or compassionate enough; males do not look upon the teaching profession as high status; low salaries; and so on. He also goes on to write about how boys look up to male role models. So in his writing he describes that males can be a large factor in helping many students succeed. Male teachers can create good bonds with young male students because they "speak the same language" or have the same likes, so to speak. All of his writing was backed by research.

In conclusion, we set out to find reasons why there is a gender gap, and from our survey's results we see a gender gap. When you think of all the teachers in a school, there can be 25, 30, or more. We saw from our data the majority of participants see fewer than eight male teachers in their schools. This gives us hard proof that there is a shortage of male teachers. In our research we wanted to figure out what are some explanations as to why more elementary teachers are female. From our results and answers that we received, we now see that much of it deals with how men view the profession. A stereotype, such as teaching is a woman's profession, is the main reason men do not get into elementary education. On the other side of that argument, many believe that males are not caring or compassionate enough to work with children. This is why many speculate that most males in the teaching profession are in secondary education. Men need to be pushed into becoming future elementary educators because they have a lot to bring to the table. We found that many teachers believe students, mostly boys, need an extra male role model in their day. The problem of the gender gap we see in our schools is a problem that should be corrected. Men just have a problem of overcoming many stereotypes that surround the teaching profession.

SOURCES

http://gpschools.schoolwires.net/1767101027124513700/lib/17671010271245131700/2010-11%20Annual%20Reports/PA25%20North%202010-11.pdf

http://www.greatschools.org/find-a-school/school-visit/35-the-achievement-gap-is-your-school-helping-all-students-succeed.gs

http://nces.ed.gov/nationsreportcard/pdf/stt2011/2012454MI8.pdf

http://www.coro.org/atf/cf/%7Bf3d20884-27f3-49f1-a026-e8ca36eb0544%7D/
ACHIEVEMENT%20G APJPG

http://1.bp.blogspot.cam/_TcU1IJOo18E/TlaGYPSEhfl/AAAAAAAAAVo/_bBsWE6TaAw/s640)/
School-Test-Poverty-Gaps.jpg

Google Images

www. city-data.com

Research Project #2: Inclusive Teachings in the Classroom

Ryan McCombs, Zach Rondot, and Madison Mitchell

ABSTRACT

According to the IDEA Amendments of 1997, students with physical and cognitive disabilities are entitled to the general education curriculum that all other students have access to. Because of this, educators will need to work to make special modifications to lesson plans and classroom environments. Educators have access to an Individualized Education Program for any student that qualifies for any alternative teaching methods that they will be requiring. According to the Core Democratic Values placed by our forefathers, all individuals require to be treated with the same rights and with the same equal opportunity. At this time we believe that students with physical or cognitive disabilities that are being educated in the school systems are receiving accommodations that they deserve and are being given the same education as a student without any disabilities would be receiving. We will be interviewing K–5 educators and administration regarding how they meet the accommodations of all students in both the school and in the classroom.

INTERVIEWED

- 3rd Grade Teacher
- 5th Grade Teacher
- Associate Superintendent/Former Principal
- Special Education Teacher
- Future Teachers

INTERVIEW SURVEY QUESTIONS

- What is your perspective on inclusion?
- What actions have been taken to accommodate all students in the classroom?
- To what extent has inclusion changed classroom instruction?
- What role do parents play in facilitating inclusion in your classroom/school?
- How effective are Individualized Education Programs (IEPs) for students that qualify for them?

- What training does your district provide in order to educate teachers to better provide inclusive instruction in their classrooms?

WHAT THE EXPERTS SAID

What is your perspective on inclusion?

- Perspective: Practicing Classroom Teachers (2)
  - "Whenever a student is able to be part of the regular class and work and share with peers, it is a positive experience for that child." —6th grade teacher
  - "I have had students with a variety of emotional, physical, and mental challenges as members of our class, and, most generally, the class benefits greatly by learning from and assisting in the education of those children." —3rd grade teacher
  - "I believe that inclusion is a positive thing for the classroom in that children of differing abilities/needs learn to work together, acknowledging differences in a positive way." —5th grade teacher

- Perspective: Associate Superintendent (1)
  - "Students with disabilities benefit by being exposed to the same rigorous curriculum content and instruction as their non-disabled peers."
  - "The general education students often benefit by gaining a greater understanding of students with disabilities and hopefully, develop skills to appropriately interact and support their peers who have physical or cognitive disabilities."

- Perspective: Future Classroom Teachers (3)
  - "I think that it is beneficial to all the students as long as the teacher does it correctly."— Future student 1
  - "I think inclusion is fair and beneficial to the students."—Future student 2
  - "I used to believe in full inclusion. Now, after having been in the classroom, full inclusion for ALL students is good in theory but horrible in practice."—Future student 3

WHAT WE FOUND

- We found that educators and administrators believe that being able to have an inclusive classroom, school, and district are a necessity for both students with disabilities and students without disabilities.
- Inclusion can be a positive experience for both students with disabilities and students without disabilities because of the different types of experiences they gain from each other.

What actions have been taken to accommodate all students in the classroom?

- Perspective: Special Education Teacher (1)

CLASS ASSIGNMENTS

- "I'm not sure if it is safe to say that all of the actions have been taken to promote success on all levels of inclusion."
- "Some actions that have taken place are putting resource teachers inside of the general education classes to help with the teaching of multiple students. Another action is to have lessons adapted to promote learning for all students, regardless of educational level."

- Perspective: Practicing Classroom Teachers (2)
  - "I, as well as most teachers I know, have shortened lessons, provided extra adult or student support, provided for additional time, restructured the physical environment, and given instruction and opportunities for completing assignments in a variety of formats with more focus on specific modalities."—5th grade teacher
  - "Para-pro support and team-teaching with a Special Ed. teacher is essential in making inclusion a success. Some districts are requiring the push-in model, and I believe that this is necessary and essential in order for inclusion to be successful."—3rd grade teacher

- Perspective: Associate Superintendent(1)
  - "The more a school or classroom can 'mirror' the 'real world,' the better the environment is for students to truly be more prepared for the 'real world.'"
  - "Students, teachers, support staff (paraprofessionals, secretary, lunchroom staff, etc.), and parents gain a greater understanding of people with disabilities, which in turn improves interactions, patience, and empathy."

- Perspective: Future Classroom Teachers (3)
  - "Giving different directions, different tests, reading the test to students, different reading books, less problems, less challenging problems."—Future student 1
  - "When I am planning lesson plans that I am going to teach to students I know, I make some modifications for certain students."—Future student 3
  - "I do not know"—Future student 2

To what extent has inclusion changed classroom instruction?

- Perspective: Practicing Classroom Teachers (2)
  - "Inclusion has changed classroom instruction in the following ways ... It is now a MUST to accommodate and facilitate learning for ALL, regardless of need, ability, etc. ... ."—3rd grade teacher
  - "With the new teacher evaluation laws in Michigan, teachers need to find a way to reach and demonstrate growth for all students."—3rd grade teacher
  - "Our certification claims that we are able to teach all students in certain grade levels in specific subject areas. That means we need to meet the expectations by learning every-

thing we can to accommodate students so that they can have an equal opportunity to learn."— 5th grade teacher

- Perspective: Associate Superintendent (1)
  - "Inclusion set the ground work for differentiated instruction. In the general classroom, now we are differentiating instruction to meet the needs of all students."
  - "We are working within a Response to Intervention (Rtl) model which requires modifications, re-teaching, small group and other interventions within the general education classroom for ALL students to learn/achieve. Progress monitoring and achievement data then drives the need for additional instructional support outside of the general education classroom."

WHAT WE FOUND

Inclusion has changed the structure and approach to classroom learning. It has opened the eyes of teachers and administrators to create differentiated instruction for individual learning styles. Inclusion puts more pressure on the classroom teacher to facilitate learning for every student in the class.

What role do parents play in facilitating inclusion in your classroom/school?

- Perspective: Special Education Teacher (1)
  - "I think if students are to succeed in an inclusive classroom, parents have to promote growth and learning in such away that the students know what to expect from each day."
  - "Parents may have to be more involved with learning outside of the classroom."
  - "A problem with that is there is a good chunk of parents who either don't have time to help their kids, or their kids are learning at a higher level than they ever did."

- Perspective: Practicing Classroom Teachers (2)
  - "Parents are involved in the IEPC setting as we set and agree on goals and level of support for their individual child."— 3rd grade teacher
  - "Many parents bring in advocates in order to make sure the needs of their child are best being met."— 3rd grade teacher
  - "They provide education to us in the form of frequent meetings and/or even self-made booklets or pamphlets to help us become more understanding and appreciative or some very unique needs and situation." — 5th grade teacher
  - "Other times, parental involvement is nearly non-existent. In those cases, we work with our principal, staff, and other agencies to iearn what best practices are and what resources can support our teaching with students ."— 5th grade teacher

- Perspective: Future Classroom Teachers (3)
  - "To make sure that the student is doing his or her work and homework. Going over homework or tests could help the students."— Future student 1

CLASS ASSIGNMENTS

- "Parents are team members and their help and support is important to help children in their education."—Future student 2
- "I don't know yet."—Future student 3

WHAT WE FOUND

- According to the educators and administrators, many of the parents in their schools are willing to help educate each other about their child's disabilities.
- Because of this, students with a supportive home life will benefit from this, and receive an education that they deserve getting.
- The students that do not receive the support they need from their parents will usually result in gaining support from other resources that the school will supply.

How effective are Individualized Education Programs (IEPs) for students that qualify for them?

- Perspective: Special Education Teacher(1)
  - "I feel the effectiveness of the IEP depends a lot on the effectiveness of the teachers surrounding that student. Special Education teachers can write a great IEP that will take care of the specific needs of that student whether it is in accommodations, or if it means having solid goals and objectives that will drive the student's learning."
  - "There are many times that the IEP is not the problem; the problem lies with the lack of execution of the IEP. As someone with a Special Education background, I feel there is a great amount of responsibility that is left on the Special Educator who must make sure the IEP is executed to its fullest potential."
  - "The most important part of the actual IEP document, and the IEP meeting, is what happens after."

- Perspective: Practicing Classroom Teachers (2)
  - "I believe that IEPs are becoming more effective in that the goals MUST now be linked and demonstrate student growth."—3rd grade teacher
  - "I think that IEPs are valuable when students qualify because they provide us with goals, methods to reach those goals, and tracking to see if students meet those goals."—5th grade teacher
  - "They also clarify the extent of support a student will receive from the resource room teacher. That enables teachers to find other resources and/or people who can help us help the child achieve to their highest ability level 3."—5th grade teacher

*What training does your district provide in order to educate teachers
to better provide inclusive instruction in their classrooms?*

- Perspective: Special Education Teacher(1)
  - "Looking at the teaching population as a whole, there was not as much push and opportunity to educate teachers on inclusion. I felt that it was more of my responsibility as the Special Education teacher to make sure that I was there for my students and help their General Education teachers in preparation for teaching in an inclusive setting."
  - "I will say I worked with some teachers who truly understood, and did a great job at promoting success, but I also worked with some where they set their own pace and whoever was left behind was left behind."

*What training does your district provide in order to educate teachers
to better provide inclusive instruction in their classrooms?*

- Perspective: Practicing Classroom Teachers (2)
  - "We have not received official training in recent year … We are hoping that with our new Special Education director, the regular classroom teacher will get additional training and support on how to implement best practices with our special needs population."– 3rd grade teacher
  - "I personally have taken post-master classes that were based on inclusion and writing/implementing IEPs and the law(s) that accompany them."– 3rd grade teacher
  - "Our specific district does not provide a great deal of resources in this area. Personally, I have done much of my own investigating through taking classes, reading research, talking with competent and qualified adults."– 6th grade teacher

WHAT WE FOUND

Minimal training has been provided to assist classroom teachers to transition into using more inclusive strategies. Laws state that teachers must keep up professional development practices, which may sometimes include strategies for things such as differentiated instruction and IEPs. Many teachers do not feel their districts have done enough to train teachers efficiently.

OUR RECOMMENDATIONS

School districts must train their educators to meet the needs of their students. All educators must have plans in place for every student that has a disability in their classroom. Educators must make classrooms inclusive to benefit both students with disabilities and students without disabilities. Educators need to get parent involvement from all students, not just parents of disabled students. The more involvement in and out of the classroom, the better the learning experience can be for all parties. IEPs must be looked at multiple times throughout the year, to make sure that the student is gaining the educational experience that they are entitled too.

CONCLUSIONS

In conclusion, we have learned that many educators think that inclusive classrooms are a necessity for learning. We believe that the training needed to help educators provide an inclusive classroom is inadequate for the students and for the school. At this time we believe that students with physical or cognitive disabilities that are being educated in the school systems are receiving accommodations that they deserve, but can also be inadequate for their learning experience. Educators are doing their best to accommodate all of their students but at times they do not have the support from the parents, school, and school district. When looking at inclusion in the classroom, we believe that it must be done with help from everyone involved: educators, school, school district, and most of all, family support.

REFLECTION (SAMPLE)

Our research has given me a much greater understanding of the financial difficulties that college students and graduates are facing. In that regard I am more familiar with the financial woes of my peers, along with some of the struggles that they will be facing as they attempt to leave college and enter the workforce. I feel as though the research process also provided me with an opportunity to hone my researching skills, particularly in the areas of collecting and analyzing data. I learned a great deal while making a survey with useful questions, and I learned even more while interpreting the information that the survey provided.

I think that the research process itself will be very helpful in my future classroom. Teachers never finish their education, and this assignment was a way for me to further educate myself through the use of extensive research. The assignment also allowed me to spend some time working with a group of peers, which will be extremely useful as an educator. Teachers are supposed to work together in order to be more effective, and any opportunity to work with a group of future educators, as was the case with this assignment, is a positive experience that will be relevant in the future. I think that preparing for the presentation will prove to be useful as well. We found a tremendous amount of information, but, like teachers, we had to sort through that information and determine what needed to be shared with the class. We also had to test that information to make sure that it was accurate, which is another skill that will be useful to have in the classroom.

Since the members of the group did learn from this assignment, I do think that having inquiry-based lessons can benefit elementary students. It gives students an opportunity to research something that they are interested in, and I feel as though students do best when they're allowed to make significant decisions for themselves. A project like this one also allows students to go beyond the "surface level" of a particular topic. Our research gave the group a rather in-depth understanding of the content, and providing students with an opportunity to really sit down and master some material is a very useful experience for them to have. Doing an inquiry-based project can also help students develop their communication skills. This project alone required the group to communicate with one another to arrange meetings, write an abstract and reflection, speak to others to receive information, and create a presentation to share with the class. Any project that can help students in so many different ways seems to be absolutely essential.

The project did involve significant contributions from each member of the group. The group spent several hours meeting in the library while collecting data and creating a presentation. Each group member also spent time researching the project on an individual basis. The creation and analysis of the survey also took up a period of time, and so did the initial draft and revision of the abstract. Though it is difficult to place the amount of time spent on this project in hours, as much of it was done on an individual basis and not at any one set time, the group as a whole spent many hours researching and interpreting the information that was found in order to provide the class with an interesting and accurate presentation that reflected what was found throughout the inquiry process.

Research Project #3: Intolerance

Victoria Pendred and Elizabeth Schnepp

ABSTRACT

Millions of people have been extinguished globally due to intolerance. In an effort to extinguish this intolerance, we Americans promote our nation as a land of the free and accepting. But is it? We aimed our research at the intolerance of Americans throughout history to see if we have become the accepting nation we promote. We looked at particular events from 1692 throughout 2012. For this project we compared and contrasted a variety of historical events that have occurred in American history that emanated from intolerance, including the Salem witch trials, slavery, Japanese encampment in WWII, the McCarthy trials, the Civil Rights movement, and post 9/11. We chose these historical events because they show how society moves through different instances and targets of intolerance. We looked at each period and who they were intolerant of, the extent to

CLASS ASSIGNMENTS

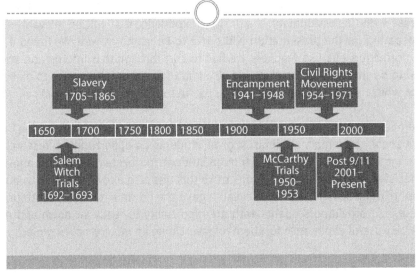

which the intolerance was invigorated, and the period's resolution, if one existed. We used primary sources from the time periods, looked at current events, and compared the events and resolutions from each time period. We have found through our research that even though modern Americans strive to be tolerant of all people, intolerance is still prevalent and perpetual.

DEFINITION OF TOLERANCE

"Today we tend to view tolerance as a double edged proposition. On the one hand it implies begrudging, almost unwilling and ungraceful acceptance of uncomfortable ideas and opposing points of view, while on the other it calls for persistent effort at understanding and a willingness to work with a diversity of ideas, free from bigotry and prejudice."

Who Can Be Intolerant?
- Citizens and Government
- Citizens can be intolerant of each other
- The government reinforces these intolerances by passing laws
- Trends of Intolerance
  - Prejudice
  - Traumatic event
  - Fear

Timeline of Presentation

Salem Witch Trials
- 1692–1693
- 24 people were hanged, crushed under rocks, or died in prison
- Causes:
  - Possessed children
  - Religion
  - Social and economic divisions

Slavery
- 1705–1865
- Africans were thought of as sub-humans and as property
- Causes:
  - Power
  - Prejudice

WWII Encampment
- 1941–1948
- Japanese Americans were confined to an internment camp
- Causes:
  - Bombing Pearl Harbor
  - Prejudice

McCarthy Trials

- 1950–1953
- People were blacklisted and interrogated because they were thought to be Communists or Communist sympathizers
- Causes:
  - McCarthy wanted reelection
  - WWII
- 320 artists blacklisted. It stopped when he started accusing people in the military

Civil Rights Movement

- 1954–1971
- African Americans were trying to earn their rights after being segregated and murdered
- Causes:
  - KKK
  - Prejudice

Post 9/11

- After the terrorist attacks on September 11, 2001, people started to become afraid of the "Muslim terrorists." A lot of Americans identified Muslim Americans as terrorists. Muslim Americans were connected with the Muslim hijackers
- Causes:
  - 9 /11 attack and consequent war in Middle East
  - Prejudice
- "Iraqi Woman Beaten to Death in California, Hate Crime Suspected" – ABC News

SUMMARY

- We picked isolated events in society; however, it is continually present and there were more than what we could talk about. For example: Native American Oppression, International Intolerance (Nazi) and Latin America
- We predict that intolerance will always be a problem but will switch to different groups; it is always going to be with us.

Why should we teach this to our students?

- It is an important part of our history and a part of our world today
- Children notice differences at a young age and learn stereotypes that must be addressed
- Teaching tolerance to students can help to reduce negative acts (i.e. hate crimes and bullying)
- Creates a more cooperative and safe environment in the classroom where children can express their differences without fear of discrimination.

WHAT WE LEARNED

- "You don't have to accept other people, but you do have to tolerate them."—Unknown
- The trends of intolerance: traumatic event and prejudice
- More in-depth information on the events we researched for the project
- Incorporated a variety of primary sources into our research, analysis, and presentation

REFERENCES

Bare Naked Islam. (2010, February 28). Retrieved from http://barenakedislam.com/2010/02.

Blah32123. (2008, March 28). *Japanese Internment Camps During WWII* (Video file). Retrieved from Youtube database.

Catechetical Guild (1947). *Is This Tomorrow: America Under Communism* (Comic Book). Retrieved from Wikipedia database.

Challenging Media. (2007, February 1). R*eel Bad Arabs: How Hollywood Vilifies a People.* Retrieved March 25, 2012 from Youtube website: http://www.youtube.com/watch?v=Ko_N4BcalPY.

Hoffman. B. A. (1999, February 22). *George Washington and Toleration.* Retrieved March 25, 2012 from http://www.msa md.gov/msa/stagser/s1259/131/html/gw22299spech.htm.

Hopper, K. (2011). *Timeline of Civil War.* Retrieved March 25, 2012, frmm http://civilwarinvirginia. wordpress. com/page/7/.

Jones, J., Wood. P. H., Borstelmann, T., May, E. T., & Ruiz, V. L. (2008). *Created Equal: A. Social and Political History of the United States: Vol. 2. From 1865.* New York: Pearson Education.

Katrandjiam, O. (2012, March 25). *Iraqi Women Beaten to Death in California: Hate Crime Suspected.* Retrieved March 25, 2012, from http://abcnews.go.com/blogs/headlines/2012/03/iraqi-woman-beaten-to-death-in-california-hate-crime-suspected/.

Linder, D.O. (2009, September). *Salem Witch Trials 1692.* Retrieved March 25, 2012, from http://law2. unkc.edu/faculty/projects/ftrials/salem/SALEM.HTM.

Make the World a Better Place. (2011, March 10). Retrieved March 25, 2012, from http://www.richard-silverstein.com/tikun_olam/tag/anti-arab/.

MumbhaiMBBS. (2007, April 14). *Allah Made Me Funny* (Video file). Retrieved from Youtube database

Primary Source: Documents in U.S. History (Vol. 1). (2009). Upper Saddle River: Pearson.

US Slave. (2011, May 6). Retrieved March 24, 2012, from http://usslave.blogspot.com/2011/05cotton-in-global-economy-mississippi.html.

World War Two Propaganda Posters. (n.d.). Retrieved March 25, 2012, from http://sharenator.com/World_War_Two_Propaganda Posters/#/american_3_World_War_Two_Propaganda_Posters-11.html

WWII Propaganda. (n.d). Retrieved March 25, 2012, from http://apusb.wikispaces.com/WWII+propaganda.

Documenting Learning in Social Studies Through Reflections

How do you know learning has taken place?

Give students ownership of learning.

Traditionally, students have been schooled to be passive recipients of learning and learning for the grade as their ultimate goal for being in the classroom. Passive learning results in boredom, and low or no motivation.

In social studies students should be given the opportunity to reflect on the process and articulate in their own words the knowledge, skills, and dispositions they have developed as a result of completing the research project. The reflective activity helps students make sense of what they learned and feel a sense of accomplishment. After completing their projects, students in my Social Studies Methods reflected in writing on how completing the assignment helped them gain knowledge, master skills, and develop democratic dispositions.

In their own words students in my cohorts class noted what they liked about social studies:

Student #1   Now I know that social studies is not just about teaching specific lessons on community or history, it is about doing research to find that information out. I learned that I cannot only use lesson plans to teach social studies, I need to be able to do hands-on things with my students.

Student #2   Social studies is not just history, but is as important as any math or science instruction because it will determine how a person is informed about the world in which he or she lives ... When I felt overwhelmed with my research, I thought about what it would be like to be doing this for the first time and how scared and upset I would have felt.

Student #3   I learned about the value of using inquiry-based instruction. I was much more engaged in this type of learning and had responsibility in my learning. It was a powerful tool to learn about social studies.

Student #4   I never really had good experiences with group projects, but I very much enjoyed working with people who also want to be elementary school teachers. I think this project was very worthwhile and I enjoyed doing it.

Student #5

Our project served us well and gave us an experience that is uncommon in many college classes. We directed our own learning in this project and we got [back] what we put into the process. Our work was rewarded by ourselves. At the same time we were still guided and were encouraged to ask for help or advice. Overall, the inquiry project provided much more than lecture ever could.

Student #6

During the completion of this assignment I learned that team work is very difficult. While it is nice to have teammates to work with and discuss projects with, it is always difficult to find times to work together, and sometimes we got frustrated with one another when we were trying to put the entire project together. Because of this, I will always remember that group work can be difficult and as a future educator I should always remember that and take it into consideration when having group work in my classroom. I will definitely apply this to future classrooms by having students work in groups on projects to build on communication and group working skills needed in school as well as in life.

Student #7

I really loved that project and learned so much about myself. It not only taught me that I can work together and get along with different members of my group without conflict or having to do everything myself, but it also taught me just how important my voice is when it comes to social networking. This project will be one that I remember forever and it really introduced me to not only how important it is to be social and get along with others to get information but how to present myself in a professional way to share findings.

Student #8

I think I really grew as a person from surveying people. I learned that questions have to be neutral, especially in the classroom; you do not want students to feel like they cannot respond because you do not agree. I learned to embrace all opinions; it makes for interesting debates and conversations to hear and be open to all sides. This is great for classrooms.

Student #9

The information that can be derived from an inquiry project is worthwhile and valuable, but the process is very involved and requires hard work to be successful.

Student #10

Researching and interviewing on this topic helped us realize our own beliefs for teaching and our goals that we want to implement when we do teach children. We have an even better understanding of our duties as a teacher . I realized that quality time is vital, as it is very difficult to meet together because of everyone's schedules. I also learned that I need to be more confident and independent. I was always unsure about my suggestions and ideas and was sometimes hesitant to bring the ideas to the table. If I were doing this project for my class, I know that I would be just like Dr. Adewui for kids to lean on. I know that there are a lot of times when students get irritated and/or stressed out with big projects/assignments and need someone to get them back on track and focused so they can produce a valuable project.

Student #11

I learned the importance of teamwork. It is important to be able to step up and hold yourself responsible for what you are working on so that you can be proud of your final product.

Student #12

This project was definitely a bit frustrating. I felt like at times I was the only one taking it seriously. I found the project very beneficial and the information that I found will help me out in the future.

Student #13

As a future teacher, letting students do research on their own on particular topics will help in their overall learning experience. Having students be in control of the way they research and by giving them freedom, students will have more fun and most likely learn more than just being talked at.

Student #14

The biggest lesson that I learned during this whole project process was how to ask inquiry questions the correct way and how to evaluate the questions from different angles. Being able to write inquiry questions is going to help me in not only my social studies instruction but also in every subject area that I am going to be teaching in my future classroom. I feel that our research really opened our eyes to what the students really think about school and what they feel is their best subject.

Student #15

Participating in SRCEE at Central Michigan University was a very exciting and valuable experience for me. I never presented a research/inquiry project at a college event before and [being] given this opportunity was very eye opening.

Student #16

With hours of extensive research and working with my group, I feel that I learned a lot from doing this project. I feel that this is a great way to wrap up my first set of cohorts for the teacher education program. This project has given me confidence that I will be a good teacher some day and will try my hardest to make my assignments hands-on.

CLASS ASSIGNMENTS

Student #17

This was a fun experience because we were able to share our knowledge with others. Although this project was a lot of work, it was a great learning experience that taught me more than a textbook or lecture ever could. By throwing myself into the topic and being an active learner, I was able to learn more and retain more than if I just read and researched the topic.

Student #18

This inquiry project taught me a lot about how much fun social studies can be. It also showed me how much students can learn from completing an inquiry project of their own. By allowing the students to pick a topic that interests them and is also related to social studies , the students will learn a lot. It is already well established that students learn more and better when they are provided with choice, and I think an inquiry project like my group and I created is the perfect way to allow students the freedom and choice to pick a project of their own.

Student #19

I learned that doing a project like [one of] this magnitude takes a lot of hours to complete, which is why I would probably do a similar yet easier project in my class.

Student #20

I learned that being a group leader could be frustrating at times. Trying to work around four individual schedules can be difficult and group meetings can be useless unless there is a previously decided agenda. I also learned that not everything is always going to go as planned. The way we set up this project I felt that every group member was participating and things were being done equally; however, when it came time to do the actual work, certain group members were not accountable and did not do the work they said they would. Despite the drama within this project, I was able to gain a lot of wonderful knowledge about how to handle stress within the classroom.

Student #21

One of the most difficult aspects of this inquiry project was on choosing a topic. Each of us had a variety of good ideas that we wanted to focus on, so it was hard narrowing the choices down and deciding on a topic everyone was happy about. I liked the idea of focusing our inquiry project on year-round schooling because it is definitely something that could affect me as a future educator, and it is a topic I am pretty unfamiliar with. I enjoyed presenting our inquiry project at SRCEE because it gave me a chance to share with others what I learned. The most important lesson I learned as a result of this that will guide my social studies decisions in my future classroom is that being informed about public policy and social issues is extremely important to the role you play in society.

Student #22

It was different and refreshing to work outside of the classroom and to use the ideas and surveys from people around campus. This project brought a sense of connection to my university. I also enjoyed completing something for class that I cared about and would be able to use.

Student #23

I enjoyed the freedom that the project offered. There was a basic format in place but students were free to push the boundaries and explore the reasoning as well as teaching skills. The only road block, hiccup, snafu, problem, or whatever else one could call it of the assignment was the group dynamic. It is hard to pick out four people who approach an assignment in a similar fashion as oneself. Different students have different ways of approaching projects. Some like to put assignments off; others do not. I have never been one to procrastinate. To prevent our group from arguments, frustration, and diminished work as a result of stress, two groups were formed.

Student #24

Initially a student may think this is tedious work and that they just want to get through it; one will come to realize how much there is to be learned from this and that it is actually fun. I loved this experience and love my peers that I worked with.

Student #25

It has been a good experience overall and I feel I have learned a lot about myself. I feel like I know more how I work and the type of people who I work well with. I am also learning to deal with working with people who I do not necessarily work well with. This is just as important because in life, you do not always get your groups, and being stressed out through an entire project will not do anybody any good either.

Student #26

The lesson I learned is that a student can learn a lot from completing an inquiry project. Not only does a student learn that a particular issue has great effects and consequences to all members of society, but that there are great benefits to questioning these issues and being informed about them.

Student #27

This project was enjoyable because it was the largest and most detailed I have done in college so far.

Student #28

The project revealed to me that social studies is everywhere around us. While we were busy working together creating a project for class, we were actively participating in socials studies by developing social relationships.

Student #29

I feel like this whole experience has been so wonderful. I love that I had the opportunity to be a researcher and found out things about education system that I had never known. This project has given me a deeper appreciation for the U.S. education system and the changes it has gone through. Gathering the research and creating the PowerPoint was time consuming but I felt like it was time well spent. This project has impacted how I think about teaching. I have learned that it is so important to give students the opportunity to discover and explore areas of social studies on their own. Rather than just being lectured to about the U.S. education system, I taught myself. I was able to use my own abilities and talents to help myself become more knowledgeable about the education.

In their own words below, four students in my cohorts class reflected on their social studies research projects:

RESEARCH PROJECT REFLECTION #1

At the onset of this project, I assumed that this project would be similar to all the research projects that I have completed in the past. Instead, I found that this experience afforded me a tremendous insight into the manner in which social studies research should be conducted by students. I also realized the impact that this type of group work and inquiry-based learning can have on the individuals involved in the study.

Before I participated in this project, I thought research entailed being assigned a topic, or choosing from a set of topics that were selected by the instructor. I also believed that the method of conducting the research was to simply find information on the Internet or in reference materials, and then to compile the information to create a report.

This project was enlightening, because I realized that research could be much more engaging if the students were to select the topic, determine the means of researching that topic, work cooperatively to carry out the research, and draw conclusions about the data. I found that I was actually excited about doing this research rather than finding it to be a chore, because I was interested in the outcome of this investigation. As a team we had chosen the topic, and I wanted to know the answer to our hypothesis.

I also learned that research could be accomplished through a collaborative effort. The experience of working in groups adds another component to expanding students' knowledge of social studies. After all, this area of the curriculum entails the study and interaction of people. What better way is there to look at the interrelationships of people than to work with others?

Taking research out of the classroom and into the world around us not only makes social studies more interesting, it also emphasizes that social studies is about studying people, values, and how our democratic society functions. While we can learn about facts and concepts in a textbook, it is through real experiences that we truly learn about the society around us and the problems, issues, and concerns of the people in that society. I now realize that social studies cannot really be taught from a text, but rather it must be experienced through interactions with the world around us.

In regards to dispositions, this research project gave me ample opportunity to work on the skills that I will need as a future educator. At this level of my education, I don't believe that I have achieved true mastery of any given skill. However, this assignment has afforded me the chance to achieve a high level of accomplishment in several areas.

Initiative was an important aspect of this project. The entire project involved working independently with limited supervision from our instructor and without a given set of resources. This entailed creating our own subject to research, finding a means to research that subject, and carrying on the investigation. As a group member, I had to work independently to fulfill my responsibilities. I also took it upon myself to make all the arrangements to sign up our group for the conference. I feel that throughout this project I took the initiative to get things accomplished. I created the initial idea for our research, and I took on a leadership role throughout the project. I made sure that the project continued to move forward, and I made the arrangements when we were to meet for collaborations.

One of my strengths is that I have an inquiring nature and I often probe issues, questions, and problems. This project was an exercise in critical thinking and it gave me a chance to excel in this area. I posed a question that was the prompt for our research. As a group we applied a method for conducting research to attempt to answer that question, and we drew conclusions based on those findings.

This project gave me another opportunity to work on collaboration. I feel that I now have attained skills that will help me to be a more effective member of a group. While it may have been necessary for me to assume a leadership role in order to keep the project moving forward, I did many things to help others to successfully contribute to the project. I provided guidance, gave feedback, and offered suggestions. I listened to the other group members' input and encouraged them in their endeavors. Most importantly, I worked toward a cohesive union of ideas and effort.

This assignment has prepared me for my future classroom in three ways. First and foremost, this lesson has modeled that an instructor's role is not to simply instruct students in the subject matter, but that the instructor should facilitate learning instead. The students will teach themselves if given opportunities through guided group work and experiences. This type of learning is more likely to have an impact on them than memorizing information from a text. I know that I will remember everything that I learned by performing this research, because I was emotionally and intellectually engaged. Secondly, inquiry-based learning is an effective means of teaching students, especially if the questions are posed by the students themselves. Students will be highly motivated to learn if they want to know the answers. I know I truly cared to know if students were learning through taking part in student government, so I worked toward finding the conclusion. Finally, I learned that for social studies to be meaningful it has to have connections with the real world. If I had read a bunch of statistics in a text about findings that related to students' involvement with student government in connection to their knowledge of government in society, it would have been just information. Reading questionnaires and seeing the students' actual thoughts in writing had a greater impact on me. There was an emotional connection. Students need that form of involvement to learn about social studies, because it is a human endeavor, not just dry statistics.

As I have mentioned throughout this paper, social studies is the study of the world around us, and the learning experience should not be confined to readings from a textbook and teacher lectures. If the association that students have between social studies and learning is memorized facts, then they are missing the entire concept of social studies.

I feel that research projects would be highly beneficial to students, particularly if students choose their own research topics. With this type of inquiry-based learning, students are seeking answers to questions that they want to know. The motivational factor for learning is greater, because the subject matter engages the students. We don't want students to just learn about the subject matter at hand, we want them to become excited about learning. In this way, they will become lifelong learners. By giving them positive learning experiences, they will be inspired to continue to seek similar experiences in the future.

Research takes students beyond the classroom environment and out into the world around us. This is particularly true if students are using a method of investigation that involves interactions with other people, such as interviews, surveys, and observations. Could there be a more appropriate way to study the world around us than hands-on experiences in that environment? Even if students are doing research via texts and the Internet, they are still learning through a means that is outside the realm of the classroom lecture.

It would be highly beneficial to a diverse group of learners if research projects were allowed to be presented in a variety of forms, such as we did in our class. This enhances the learning experience for each individual or group, as well as creating a more exciting learning environment for the entire class. We enjoyed the many different types of projects in our own class. Diversity should be an important aspect in studying social studies. What could be a better means to express human diversity than to allow everyone to communicate their ideas in ways that best suit their learning style?

In conclusion, I think that this research project emphasized all the ideals that we learned throughout the semester about teaching social studies. Students are going to learn far more through activities that engage them in learning than through lecture and text reading.

RESEARCH PROJECT REFLECTION #2

Final Reflection

For this research/inquiry project my group and I decided to take an in-depth look at the use of Individualized Education Plans (IEPs) and their use in the general education classroom and the effects of inclusion. This project has helped me gain new knowledge, skills, and dispositions by taking part in this inquiry-based project. By interviewing current practicing classroom teachers, a special education teacher, a superintendent/former principal, and future teachers, I have gained a much greater understanding of the process of inclusion and IEPs. I now understand that an IEP is not given to any students and that there must be research and hard data before someone gets placed on an IEP. I have also learned that there is speculation about the effectiveness of IEPs within the field of education. As far as dispositions, the most important lesson I will take with me on my continual journey of becoming an effective educator is that the teaching process must be learner centered. This means that all teaching must revolve around the learner and not the other way around. It is not how the teacher wants to teach a subject; they need to teach it in ways that all students will learn the material. Especially with inclusion, all teachers will have students with special needs and disabilities and they must find a way to teach those students. With inclusion come differentiation and the idea that teachers must alter their teaching methods in order to accommodate the needs of all students. I have also gained the knowledge that districts are not doing enough to provide training for teachers on differentiating instruction for an inclusive setting. One of my future goals in education is to obtain a master's degree in Educational Leadership and become a principal or maybe even continue on to being a superintendent. The fact that administrators are not providing their teachers with enough practice and education on how to properly teach in an inclusive classroom is disturbing to me. I completely understand the lack of funding to be able to provide teachers with formal training for this, but as someone who aspires to get a degree in educational leadership, it is amazing that they don't even hold staff meetings with some type of training for inclusion. This has really opened my eyes and I will remember this as something to work on as someone who may hold an administrative position.

This assignment has prepared me as a future teacher in all aspects but specifically as a social studies teacher. From doing research, it seems that social studies can be one of the hardest subjects in which to differentiate instruction and to teach to all students. It seems this way because a lot of teachers still teach social studies in lecture format, which, for students with disabilities, makes it hard to focus and retain the information. I also feel like this gets overlooked because people always talk about how everyone needs basic math skills and writing skills every day, so they focus solely on those skills with students with disabilities. In reality, social studies teaches you how to be an active, productive, and law-abiding citizen in the world outside of the classroom, which are skills that everyone needs. Disabilities or not, the student will turn 18 at some point and if they choose, they will be able to vote. It is the job of the social studies program to educate all students on how to make informed decisions and how to act as a citizen. The first specific idea that I am going to take in my social studies teachings is to make sure to differentiate instruction so that all students are learning the same material and can leave my classroom an informed citizen regardless of ability level.

The next idea I will take from this project to my social studies classroom is that if I have a student who has an IEP, that as a responsible educator, I need to follow the plan of action that was set for the student. When we interviewed a special education teacher he mentioned, "The most important part of the actual IEP document, and the IEP meeting, is what happens after."

CLASS ASSIGNMENTS

This quote was really powerful to me because a plan can only be successful if it is properly executed. A perfect plan can be set in place for a student at an IEP meeting and in the document, but if the teachers and parents do not do their part, the student will not succeed. The second idea I will take specifically into my social studies classroom will be that, if a student has an IEP, follow it!

The third thing I will take from this research is how important the parents are in making inclusion and an IEP a successful plan of attack. Part of educating a student with disabilities is educating the parents. If the parents can help take the lessons from social studies and continue lessons in being a good citizen or making informed decisions, the process will have a much greater success rate. One teacher we interviewed said, "Other times, parental involvement is nearly non-existent. In those cases, we work with our principal, staff, and other agencies to learn what best practices are and what resources can support our teaching with students." I found this to be very important because it shows how important parental support is; however, if that is nonexistent, it does not mean you can quit on the student; it is the teacher's job to find other resources for the student so they can have the best opportunity process to learn like any other student.

I absolutely believe it is important to have students engage in historical or research-based inquiry projects. One reason I think this is important is that it puts the learning in their own hands. With much less guidance the students personalize their findings and are proud of what they have done. I believe that this makes learning much more powerful and the students will be much more likely to retain the information due to the fact that they did it on their own and were not helped through the process. Another reason I think these inquiry projects are essential is that it builds teamwork and communication skills. In doing projects like this where you are working with a team, you must be in constant communication and develop solid teamwork skills. These skills are necessary for any job and it also builds on the social studies concepts of being a good citizen and of professional etiquette. This also puts students into the leadership role in which they must become proactive in getting work done. I also think research and historical inquiry projects are important because it is different than the typical progression of learning. Far too often in classrooms, a teacher shows up with high curricular goals and then once they begin teaching, the students are not interested, so they check out. With inquiry-based projects, there is no linear model of progression for the learning to take place. The students must pick a topic, do the research all themselves, and maybe it reinforces their ideas or maybe it changes their ideas completely. Either way, it is the students who are in charge of the learning, which makes for much more meaningful learning and the retention of the information. Inquiry-based projects are also much more open-ended, giving the students the freedom to attack their topic as they would like. It does not force students to take one approach, so it gives them much more freedom in the learning process.

RESEARCH PROJECT REFLECTION #3

1. As a result of conducting this research project I have learned many things. As far as knowledge goes, I have learned a lot about the topic that we researched. We came to the conclusion that Social Studies is just not seen as important in schools anymore. I have also learned that teachers feel they are so strapped for time that that is the main reason they feel they can't teach Social Studies in the classroom. Furthermore, I have learned that teachers teach to the

standards when it comes to Social Studies topics. Some of these standards included communities, Michigan history, geography, economics, and many others. One thing that really shocked me was that some teachers reported that they didn't even have a Social Studies curriculum.

Some skills that I have learned from this research project was how to send a professional email to teachers and also how to tabulate the feedback that we got back from those teachers in order to come to conclusions about the amount of time spent on Social Studies in the classroom. After that I also had to learn the skills of putting together charts and graphs in order to present our information. I have also learned how to talk to others in a professional manner, as I had to do at the SCREE conference. It was nice to explain all of the hard work to others who were interested in finding out what we had researched. It was also helpful to have that experience in order to help me with further interviews and questioning from others.

Overall, I feel like I have gained many dispositions from completing this research project. Like I previously stated, by presenting at the SCREE conference, I really felt I gained professional knowledge and I was able to stand behind research that I had completed. I also thought that we picked a great research project because as future teachers this is something we want to make others aware of and share how easily Social Studies can be integrated into other subjects. I have also learned how to talk/email other professionals in my field that I can rely on for insight when I begin teaching (and even in my undergraduate studies). It was nice to be able to get their feedback and see what types of things to look forward to and be aware of when I begin teaching.

2. This assignment has definitely prepared me for my future Social Studies classroom. The first and foremost way is that I WILL have Social Studies in my classroom. Like I have previously mentioned, Social Studies can be integrated so easily with reading so there is no reason not to teach and celebrate Social Studies concepts and monumental holidays. Secondly, getting the responses from the questionnaires has given me an idea of what the standards are at each grade level. The teachers explained how their Social Studies curriculum was set so 2nd graders learned about communities, 4th graders Michigan History, and so on and so forth. Even though I printed out all of the standards, I never really got a chance to look over all of them, so with the teachers filling out the questionnaires and telling us about what they were teaching helped me to get an idea about what I might be teaching in my future classroom. Lastly, I have always liked doing research and I think it would fit in well in an upper elementary classroom to do some kind of research like this even if the students were to just get their research offline. I think research like this can open doors and get children interested in things they may not have thought about before. It is definitely something that I will encourage my students to do.

3. (Well I guess I should have read on before I wrote the last part on #2. Anyway, I guess I'll elaborate.) The main reason I believe it is important to have my future students take part and conduct research projects is because it can encourage them and get them interested in something that they may not have known a lot about before. It can get them excited about learning something that they are interested in. I also think that historical inquiry is important for them to learn about as well because they can find many artifacts around our community that can help their research. There is so much for the students to learn about just in their community

alone that they would be interested in if they just knew more about it. Finally, I believe that research and historical inquiry can help students learn the process of research and how to go about finding information that they might like to have. As a teacher, if I give students a project like this, they are able to learn the skills of researching a topic, presenting it, and they are learning about it in the process of their research. It can easily be integrated into technology, writing, mathematics, and reading because I could have them prepare a PowerPoint of their findings, or write a paper about what they found or even have them make a timeline or map about what they found. It can be used to supplement many other areas.

4.   Record of Time Spent on Research Project

Task	Time
Write Abstract	2 hours
Make Questionnaires/Plan	.5 hours
Send Questionnaires	4 hours
Sort Questionnaires	.5 hours
Analyze Questionnaires	4 hours
Summary of Findings	2 hours
Put Together Board	3 hours
PowerPoint/Paper	2 hours

a.   We started writing our abstract on February 21st. We completed it on the 26th and then turned it into SCREE on the 27th. It took us about 1.5 hours to figure out what we wanted to research and then compile an abstract on it. We then met with Prof. Adewui and he helped us fix some things. We then spent about a half hour fixing our abstract before we turned it in.

b.   The next thing we did was to write up a questionnaire that we would send out to teachers. It took us about a half hour to make up the questionnaires and then we put together a plan on how we were going to send out the questionnaires.

c.   Sending questionnaires took the longest of our research. We each spent 4 hours finding email addresses of teachers from all different districts and then emailing them our questionnaire. It also took a small portion of time in order to formulate an opening for our email in order to get the teachers to respond to us.

d.   After we got the questionnaires back we decided to organize them per grade so then we could start to analyze them. It took us approximately half an hour.

e.   After organizing the questionnaires we went through and read all of the responses. This took a long time as well (about 3 hours). We then took the results and started making graphs and charts with them. (1 hour)

f.   After we had all of the data charted, we wrote up a summary of our findings. We included the charts and graphs and any data we had received. We also put together quotes that teachers had said on our questionnaire as part of our research. We also researched reasons Social Studies should be taught in the elementary school and not held back until middle school. We reported our findings in our summary.

g. Next we put together our board to present at S.C.R.E.E. This took us about 3 hours to get everything organized and perfect.

h. Lastly, we organized our results into a PowerPoint and a paper. This took about 2 hours.

RESEARCH PROJECT REFLECTION #4

Through the course of this research assignment I have learned that the gender gap is prevalent in the education program and work force. From what I have learned as a result of this project is that it is going to be a difficult battle to diminish the gender gap from the field of education, but through determination and standing up for what I believe in, it can be done. I've been able to master my problem-thinking skills through this project, as well as critically thinking, in terms of social issues. I have mastered several dispositions as a result of this assignment; to name a few: critical thinking [is obviously one of them], commitment to lifelong learning is another, responsibility, emotional maturity, and responsiveness to professional feedback. I believe that I have gained a better grasp on my emotions because at times it can be difficult to work in a group setting. By doing this assignment and working with others whom I have never had any experience working with helped me gain a better understanding of responsibility and keeping my emotions together at the appropriate time(s). I've also learned how to give feedback as well as receive it, and I believe this is a disposition that should be mastered in any profession.

This assignment has prepared me as a future social studies instructor by giving me the necessary tools of inquiry. I've learned how to think critically about social issues and word questions in a manner that leads to the meaning of the topic, and to look at social issues from different perspectives. This project has prepared me as a better critical thinker because I have had to dig and research to understand why something is the way that it is, rather than assuming the answer. Critical thinking is all about deciding whether something is true or not, and whether or not to agree or disagree with that claim. This process of thinking can also be considered, in some ways, thinking about thinking, and it allows teachers to grasp a deeper understanding of their students if they can think and try to understand how their students are thinking. This project has not only helped me become a better critical thinker, but also grasp a better skill of asking questions. It can be difficult to word questions so that the answer isn't too particular but more broad and generalized. This difficult mastery, once accomplished, can create better critical thinkers in the classroom, as well as a sense of creativity due to the many answers that will be received.

I think that it is very important to the purpose of social studies education to engage my future students in research/inquiry projects because of the knowledge that is obtained as an outcome. Once the project is complete, the goal is for them to have an understanding to think more critically than they did before, comprehend/master the concept that they researched, and be able to convey their ideas. The project will help them think more critically because they will be asking questions in answer to some questions while researching; just as I did for this project. They will understand the topic that they are inquiring about as well, which will lead them to be more of a "master" in the subject than just a student. While presenting their ideas, their "mastery" of said topic will shine through, and this will help students become more confident, not only in general, but with speaking and sharing their ideas to a large group.

Time Spent on Project

Date	Amount of Time (approximately)	Details
March 18, 2012	1 hour	First group meeting; I worked on abstract.
March 23, 2012	1 hour and 30 minutes	Discussed abstract with professor; finalized abstract and turned in.
April 4, 2012	1 hour	Group meeting to discuss our plans; rough draft of survey questions.
April 6, 2012	1 hour	Worked on survey and completed; sent to teammates
April 9, 2012	2 hours	Group meeting regarding survey and collecting data; made calls and conducted survey
April 9–April 11	1 hour	Emails between teammates regarding survey results and analyzing data
April 11	1 hour	Group meeting to carry out investigation; determine each teammate's job
April 11	1 hour	Worked on PowerPoint
April 12	45 minutes	Worked on graphs
April 16	3 hours	Worked on/finalize poster board, graphs, and PowerPoint with Taylor

APPENDICES

Appendix A

Action Verbs and sample Activities in teaching a thematic unit from the 10 NCSS themes.

Desired Learning Outcomes

By the end of the unit, students will be able to:

- Interview
- Select
- Investigate
- Collect
- Analyze
- Categorize
- Create
- Discuss
- Present
- Explain
- Research
- Describe
- Compare
- Contrast
- Summarize
- Conclude
- Write
- Present

APPENDICES

Sample Activity #1

In groups you will investigate the influences of the climate and geographic conditions on people in particular regions here at home and around the globe. Collect pictures, weather forecasts, and other data from the media, magazines, YouTube etc., and identify different types of clothing, houses, food, work, sports and activities in the regions you have selected. Select 3 characteristics that distinguish people and 3 that bring them together. Analyze and categorize what is unique for each of the characteristics. Create a poster to show how the climate and geographic conditions in each place might be the cause for these differences. Present and explain your findings to the class.

Sample Activity #2

In your group, research information about the United States and then about a European and non-European country. Look for information related to beliefs, religion, food, housing, government, geography, clothing, life style and education systems. Compare and contrast the information you obtained between the three countries. Summarize your information in a written report from the point of view of a reporter and present it to the class.

Sample Activity #3

Work in groups as investigative reporters. Develop questions that you will use to learn about the cultural heritage or ancestral background of different students in the class. Collect information about the origin and meaning of the last names of students in the class. Analyze and organize the information by categories. Present your findings to the class and draw conclusions.

Sample Activity #4

In your groups, use the Internet to learn about a current event that is related to a conflict between people from the same country but with different cultural aspirations. Learn more about how the conflict is being resolved. Discuss how you think it ought to be resolved using factual information you gathered to back up your arguments. Share your findings with the class.

Sample Activity #5

In your group let each member bring or select a picture of an adult from a magazine or CNN website. Discuss and determine the approximate age of the person in the picture. Develop a time line from the time you believe the person was born. Add and describe major historical events that might have impacted that person in the picture from their younger years until old age. Speculate and explain how you think the person was affected. Present your timeline to the class.

Sample Activity #6

In your group, select a current event and look for the facts and accounts of the event from a variety of media outlets: CNN, PBS, ABC, A&E etc. Compare and contrast the accounts. Assess the credibility of the accounts and write your own account based on your information. Share your research and account with the class.

Sample Activity #7

In your group, you will collect information on current events here at home and abroad from local as well as foreign news media outlets such as BBC, RFI, etc. Organize your findings in categories and assign a label to different points of view. Create a chart to illustrate the variety of biases and points of view. Share your findings with the class.

Sample Activity #8

American businesses are sometimes blamed for exploiting undocumented workers at home and workers in poor countries through cheap labor. Items such as designer clothes, toys, and electronics are assembled by poor people in foreign countries and shipped to the United States for rich consumers. In your group you will research the issue and document your findings using a chart to compare wages from workers abroad and at home. Report your findings and conclusions to the class.

Sample Activity #9

In your group, you will identify and survey at least 10 local businesses to determine how connected they are globally. List the nature of the connections and find out about the pros and cons of each of these connections in both ways. Based on your findings, speculate and predict the future trend and its effect on local jobs. Present your findings to the class using chart, pies or tables to illustrate your evidence.

Sample Activity #10

In your group, discuss and determine what the concept of fairness means to each member of the group and then the entire group. Next you will interview a sample of at least 20–25 students representing the current demographics in the country to find out what fairness means to them. Organize the information on a chart to illustrate examples of fairness and unfairness as defined by the people interviewed. Present your findings to other students.

Appendix B

Research Project Ideas Related to Social Studies

Economics

Work with students in a given school and grade level to investigate patterns of use of credit cards.

Work with students in a given school and grade level on writing skills to obtain financing for their classroom/school or community improvement efforts.

Work with students in a given school and grade level to develop budgeting and savings skills.

Work with students in a given school and grade level to develop energy saving skills in their classroom/schools/homes.

Work with students in a given school and grade level to establish a classroom/school credit union.

Work with students in a given school and grade level to study food costs in their community stores.

Work with students in a given school and grade level to make sense of needs and wants and the consequences in going bankrupt.

Civics

Work with students in a given school to organize a fund-raising effort to support their neighbors in the community.

Work with students in a given school and grade level to organize an emergency food program.

Work with students in a given school and grade level to draft legislation to regulate quality of meals served in their cafeteria.

Work with students in a given school and grade level to develop educational materials on sound dietary habits for children.

Work with students in a given school and grade level to contact their representatives and/or businesses in their community to obtain funding and donations for specific school/classroom needs.

Work with students in a given school and grade level to organize a tutoring center in their school.

Work with students in a given school and grade level to develop resources to help tutor students with learning difficulties.

Arrange for retirees and seniors to serve as reading buddies for a given grade level in a given school.

Work with students in a given school and grade level to prepare a newsletter that publishes students concerns and suggestions in the school/in the community.

Work with students in a given school and grade level on how to write individual/group letters to their representatives.

History

Work with students in a given school and grade level to help dispel stereotypes and biases against cultural patterns of minority groups in our society.

Take students in a given school and grade level on field trip to learn about the heritage of Native Americans.

Work with students in a given school and grade level to document the history of their or a given neighborhood or city through oral history.

Collect data on the history of a given cultural practice in your city or state that undermined the core principles.

Collect and document data from private and public organizations on the achievements and contributions of minorities and developing countries to the local/state/national culture.

Develop learning strategies to help minority students understand and celebrate their own background and ancestry.

Work with students in a given school and grade level to document local folk music.

Appendix C

Technology:
Web Resources for Social Studies Teachers

For Lesson Plans:
- EDSITEment
- Library of Congress
- Teaching with Documents (National Archives)
- Social Studies Lesson Plans from U of W (Oshkosh) (Has links to multiple sites for a variety of lessons)
- MeL (you can do an advanced search for lesson plans)
- Teaching History

Other sites of interest:
- Teacher's Domain

Production and Communication

iMovie

iMovie is a video-editing application made by Apple. It is very user-friendly and easy to understand. iMovie was originally released in 1999, but has been continuously updated since. Videos can be easily uploaded from the device and compiled into a full video with theme music and captions. Editing options are available to make your video professional while also keeping it easily accessible. Once your video is complete, it can be saved on your computer or sent via email.

Dropbox

Dropbox is an application where you can upload and save pictures, docs, or videos. It automatically saves to all your computers, mobile devices, and even on the website. This way you can start a project at home and finish it at school, or vice versa. None of your stuff will ever be lost or deleted. You can have 2G for free, 100G for $9.99/month, or 200G for $19.99/month and is compatible with the iPod Touch, iPhone, iPad, Macs and PCs.

This type of tool is like a storage space. You can upload any content to it and store it as long as you want, until you need to use it again. It also allows you to share with others, whether you're a professional or not. The functions of this application are to upload and save content until it is needed elsewhere. Dropbox makes sharing really easy, too. You can send family members, teammates, or business partners links to your specific folders on Dropbox. This makes feeling connected more convenient and simple. Even if your computer breaks down or you accidentally delete a file, everything is still saved on the app. Even deleted information can still be recovered.

Splice

Splice is a video editing application that lets you combine videos, pictures, sound effects, music, transitions, borders, effects, and your own voice to make one cohesive video. Although Splice has many features, it is very convenient and easy to use. It allows users to upload their own videos, pictures and music to one project adding in title slides and transitions to help the movie flow smoothly. With splice you can easily share videos with others by posting it to facebook, YouTube, Twitter, or emailing it directly to others. This low-priced app is extremely beneficial because of its ability to edit and share videos at any place or time. Splice is available on the iPod 4/3GS and the iPod touch for free, or the full package can be purchased for $3.99.

LiveBinders

LiveBinders allows you to create and share information including documents, files, and images that can be viewed on your mobile device with teachers and students around the world. LiveBinders are great for organizing every subject and for every teacher.

Type of tool: Organizational online binder for your lesson plans.

Content: Covers a mass variety of subjects for all ages including social studies, mathematics, science, etc.

Functions: LiveBinders allows you to access others' binders and to also create and share your ideas and documents.

Skype

Skype is a free video conferencing tool that can be used on a computer or using an iDevice. It is a networking/communication tool that allows for a person to video chat with another person no matter where either person is in the world. The functions involved with Skype include face-to-face video chats with another individual, chats with multiple people at once, and also chatting via text on-screen. Skype is compatible with all iDevices (iPod touch, iPad, iPhone).

History

Today's Document *by the National Archives*

Today's Document mobile app by the National Archives is an interactive gallery of US history. This particular app, allows students to research different documents that took place on each day of the year. There are 365 different documents, one for each day of the year, allowing you to see for example what important US historical event took place on your birthday. Today's Document is compatible for both the iPad and iPod. There are buttons that allow the user to research more information on each document. There are links to other sites as well for further research. There is also a social media link, allowing the user the ability to share documents via Facebook, Twitter, etc.

DocsTeach

If you are in the need for an education application to help browse or relive the history of the United States using primary documents, DocsTeach will fulfill those needs with plenty of resources in reserve. The National Archives and Records Administration has developed a tool that allows users to explore events in United States history using the primary documents specific to topic, event, or era. This application costs $4.99 and can only be accessed through the iPad but gives the user access to thousands of historical articles, documents and other helpful resources that would be an asset to any social studies class.

Imagine reading the arrest warrant put out for Rosa Parks to get a feeling of our country just 57 years ago. DocsTeach has tools to make learning about history, government, and society unique and creative for the teacher or student. According to DocsTeach.org, "If you find an activity you want to share with your students or have created and published your own, simply provide your students with the unique web address for that individual activity. Students can complete the activity and email the results if desired" to allow to keep track of student progress (the National Archives).

The National Archives developed a free web site that allows a user to create lessons specific to the user's needs. The documents and historic information are from the National Archives, so you can be confident in their validity. After creating an account, the user can start creating activities and sharing them with colleagues and challenging their students to explore history.

American Revolution Interactive Timeline

The American Revolution is by far the most important time in American history. It symbolized when we became an independent country from Great Britain. The American Revolution History app available on the iPad is a fun and interactive view on important items, and events that took place during the war. When you first open the application you see a battle ground as the main menu with a link to explore the timeline, where you can touch objects and have them expanded; for example, one of the first items seen on the timeline is an engraved powder horn, when you touch it, it expands and looks almost life-like, accompanied by videos of the artifact that help teach what the artifact is and what its purpose was for. The artifacts that are covered in the timeline are everything from early American artwork from weapons to clothing and everyday objects. All of these features contribute to the main function of this application, which is to teach people of all ages about the changes that have occurred throughout the country's history. This application does have one downside—it is only available on the iPad, which could be inconvenient for people who can't necessarily afford to purchase one.

LineTime: Presidents Edition

LineTime: Presidents Edition is an application that allows the user to view a timeline of each president of the United States. With this timeline you can scroll across the screen in order to view the party, term, and image of each president. If you click on the image of a president, it will provide additional information by taking you to a Wikipedia article with a description of the president and various facts regarding his presidency. The app also has a search function, marked by the magnifying glass in the upper right-hand corner that allows you to enter the name of a president, rather than scrolling through the timeline. LineTime: Presidents Edition works for the iPod touch, iPhone, and iPad.

APPENDICES

Explorer: The American Museum of Natural History

An application or app for a device is supposed to make life easier for the person using it. That is exactly what this free app from theAmerican Museum of Natural History does. The app is a virtual tour guide and navigational system through the American Museum of Natural History in New York City and is compatible with the iPhone, iPad, and iPod touch devices as long as it has IOS 3.0 or later. The functions of the app take you around the whole museum from floor to floor, exhibit to exhibit; it can even give you directions to the restroom, gift shop, or cafeteria so you can never get lost. One of the features is that you can plan your whole day and what exhibits you want to see and you can check them off as you go. Share exhibits with friends and family on Twitter, Facebook, or via email. There is even a "Fossil Treasure Hunt" to make the learning experience fun for children. Choose from several guided tours or create your own custom tour; you can even bookmark places you like along the way. This app does a great job making a day at the museum fun and hassle free.

Smithsonian

This app displays information about the different museums, what they offer, and the different activities they have going on. It also gives dates and times that museums open, and information about different kinds of museums in your local area. This app makes it very easy and accessible to anyone to find different museums that they may be interested in. Users have the ability to like different museums, events, exhibitions, highlights, and collections and put them in a "favorites" folder. You are also able to look up different events for a certain day if you are looking for a special event, and you have a map option that allows you to get directions to a certain museum. This app is compatible with both the iPad and the iTouch. For the iPad, the app is called Smithsonian Channel, but it's the same thing.

Current Events

PBS Newshour

The PBS Newshour application is a very useful tool for catching the PBS Newshour at virtually any place with an internet connection whenever the user would like. The app includes various categories of news in the form of articles, videos, podcasts and pictures. The app also gives the choice of having an article read out loud or shown as a news video. When the app is opened, it shows the latest news, along with a toolbar that allows one to choose a specific category of news. This toolbar can also be edited—it includes the categories Economy, Art Beat, Podcasts, Making Sense, Science and Tech, Social Issues, World, and Legal Info. The user can choose which categories pop up on the toolbar. With that being said, this app functions as a wonderful and educational news source. Its news can also be shared with others via Twitter, Facebook, or email. It is also compatible with the iPhone, iPad, and the iPod Touch.

Maps

Google Earth

Google Earth is an interactive app that allows you to search the world. It's like the globe from your 5th grade classroom all grown up. Type in any address and zoom there in seconds, allow current location and you will always know where you are. Google Earth has many interactive tools to use, including touch activated navigation through areas you desire. It has a search bar that allows you to put in any area/address and it will zoom to that point. It also has a compass that lets you know what direction you may be going. The most interesting/creepy tool that Google Earth has is the choice of allowing Google Earth to know where your current location is; it flashes quickly to where you are, and even if you're in a building, you appear as a dot in that building.

The functions of Google Earth are worldwide satellite coverage, 3D buildings, or you can make your own, with all sorts of geographic features such as mountains, seas, rivers etc.—some of the most extensive map data, historical images, real world situations, earthquake locations and pipelines. Google Earth also can offer features on the moon and Mars.

Reference

Library of Congress

Upon clicking the Library of Congress app, visitors will see that the Library of Congress describes itself as "the world's largest library" and explains that "this application will give you a virtual tour that mirrors the Library of Congress Experience." Guests can either read the short summary or click the "explore" button at the bottom of the screen. Once the "explore" button has been selected, visitors will be brought to a list of the library's collections where a virtual tour is offered. After selecting one of the virtual tours, guests will have the option of viewing a picture and reading a description and brief history of the entitled collection. At the bottom of page there are three options to further explore the collection. These options include an audio description, visuals, and related links for more information. The audio description is the one furthest to the left; it allows guests to listen to an audio of the collection's description. The visuals can be accessed by pressing the middle icon that looks like a camera and has a vast selection of photos to look through. The icon furthest to the right brings visitors to a list of related links. These links bring guests to the Library of Congress website, which has more indepth information than the app offers. The Library of Congress app is an interactive reference resource and functions as a useful tool for anyone interested in learning more about history. It can be used as an interactive visual aid in social studies lessons; it has the potential to increase kids' interest because they can actually see the artifacts, instead of just hearing or reading about them. This app is compatible on both the iPod and the iPad, and is even available on the iPhone.

USA Factbook

The USA Factbook is a very handy application that is available for the iPod Touch, iPad,

and iPhone. Within the app are pictures of various important documents in United States history, along with transcripts of the documents. Also included are maps, information on each state, information on the flag and the national anthem, and information on the presidents. This application would be considered a resource because it contains lots of info that a person could use when doing a project or research, or a teacher could use it when creating lessons for a history class.

APPENDICES

BrainPop

BrainPop is a free educational app for grades 3 and up that allows you to learn something new quickly and easily. With BrainPop, you are able to watch a different animated video each day and then take a quiz to test your knowledge. There is a featured video each day on the home screen but you can also find videos dealing with different subjects such as science, math, health, and many others. Once you take the quiz, you can view your score and view other videos that are related to the one you just watched. There are many other functions included in this app. For example, you are able to search for a certain topic that you want, share your scores on the quizzes with others, and subscribe to brainpop.com for more access. However, this option does require a payment depending on which subscription you choose. The app is available for the iPad, iPhone, and iPod Touch.

Geotimescale

Geotimescale is an app for the iPod Touch and the iPad. This app shows every eon, era, period, epoch, and age that the earth goes through and the approximate age of the time. This app is a huge reference guide for any geology student and almost an essential guide for any geology class. "The geological time scale functions as a massive calendar, dividing the history of life into eras, periods, and epochs based on the fossil record," (Denu, 2012) and this app puts that into the hands of the student.

CPSIA information can be obtained
at www.ICGtesting.com
Printed in the USA
LVOW03s2050220816
501395LV00001B/3/P